Decentralized Finance (DeFi) & Metaverse For Beginners 2 Books in 1 2022 The Ultimate Guide On Investing In Cryptocurrency, Bitcoin, Ethereum, Smart Contracts, Blockchain Gaming, Virtual Reality, NFT And Much More

Decentralized Finance (DeFi) 2022

A Beginners Guide On Investing, Blockchain, Smart Contracts, Peer To Peer, Borrow, Save, Trade, Cryptocurrency, Bitcoin, Ethereum, Altcoin & Yield Farming

Table of Contents

Introduction

Decentralized finance refers the ecosystem of decentralized financial applications (dapps) on the blockchain.

In this ecosystem of services without an intermediary, it is possible for anyone to interact with the different protocols to ask for loans, exchange tokens or assets, create tokens that represent real estate or real assets to sell them, rent their assets in exchange for interest .... and much more.

It is a constantly evolving world that in a few years is progressing in an impressive way involving more and more projects, people and money. To operate in this decentralized set of services there is no need for authorization from a central body such as a bank.

It is transparent, verifiable and available to everyone. Today, there are many barriers that prevent all people from enjoying certain financial services. Suffice it to say that a third world citizen does not have the ability to open bank accounts easily, or ask for a loan or invest in assets.

With DeFi, no one cares who you are or where you live, the doors are open to everyone with low costs and very high security. Anyone with an internet connection can access financial services such as Dex, stablecoins, synthetic assets (stocks, indices ...), insurance ...Users maintain full control over their resources and interact autonomously with the different protocols.

In traditional finance, you must trust an institution; in decentralized finance, math has to be trusted. It is all governed by code and mathematics (code is law), upon the occurrence of such an event there is the consequence X.

No surprises or unexpected in DeFi, no account blocked for verification or investigation by a central authority. There are only the people and the protocol.

An example to understand on the fly are the DEX (decentralized exchanges).

If we want to exchange a token for another, it will be enough for us to interact with the DEX, provide our token to the Smart contract and take the corresponding token we want from the smart contract that was previously provided by another person.

1. Understanding Decentralized Finance (Defi)

Decentralized finance (Defi) is a popular blockchain-based financial infrastructure. In general, the word refers to a protocol stack that is open, permissionless, and highly interoperable and is based on public smart contract platforms such as the Ethereum blockchain. It's a more open and transparent version of present financial services. Defi isn't dependent on middlemen or centralized organizations in particular. Instead, open protocols and decentralized apps are used (DApps). Code enforces agreements, safe and verifiable transactions are performed, and approved state changes are recorded on a public blockchain.

As a result, this architecture has the ability to generate an unalterable and highly interoperable financial system with unparalleled clarity, equal access rights, and minimal need for custodians, central clearinghouses, or escrow services, as "smart contracts" can handle the majority of these functions. For example, one can buy USD-pegged assets (so-called stablecoins) on decentralized exchanges.

All Defi protocols and applications are built on smart contracts. Smart contracts are small applications that are stored on a blockchain and run concurrently by a large number of validators. The network is built in the context of public blockchains so that each participant can participate in and verify the accurate execution of each action. As a consequence, as compared to conventional centralized computing, smart contracts are relatively inefficient. Smart contracts provide a high degree of security since they always function as stated, enabling anybody to independently verify the state changes that result. When executed properly, smart contracts are highly transparent and limit the possibility of manipulation and arbitrary interference.

To understand the uniqueness of smart contracts, we must first investigate standard server-based web apps. When a person interacts with such an app, they cannot see the program's underlying logic. In addition, the user has no influence over the execution environment. Either (or both) of these could be tampered with. As a result, the user must have faith in the application service provider. Both difficulties are addressed by smart contracts, which ensure that an application runs as planned. The contract code is kept on the underlying blockchain, making it publicly accessible. The contract's behavior is deterministic, and thousands of network members process function calls (in the form of transactions) in parallel, assuring the execution's legality. When the execution causes state changes, such as account balance changes, the blockchain network's consensus rules apply, and the changes are recorded in and protected by the blockchain's state tree.

Because smart contracts have access to a wide instruction set, they are highly customizable. They may also act as a custodian for crypto assets, with completely customizable criteria for how, when, and to whom they are transferred.

This paves the way for a slew of new applications and ecosystems to emerge. For the first time, Szabo coined the term "smart contract." Szabo went on to say that many agreements might be "hidden in the hardware and software we interact with, in such a manner as to make a breach of contract expensive...for the breacher," citing a vending machine as an example. Buterin proposed a decentralized blockchain-based smart contract platform to address trust issues regarding the execution environment and enable secure execution (composability). Wood formalized the concept and implemented it under the name Ethereum. Ethereum is the most prominent smart contract platform in terms of market value, viable applications, and development activity despite various competitors.

Defi is still a niche industry with modest volumes, but this is changing rapidly. The total amount of money invested in Defi-related smart contracts has topped $10 billion. It is crucial to realize that these are not metrics for transaction volume or market capitalization; the term "value" refers to reserves held in smart contracts that may be used in various ways as described throughout this book.

How Does Defi Work?

From a technical perspective, Defi is a group of decentralized applications (dApps) primarily running on the Ethereum smart contract ecosystem that provides blockchain-based financial services without intermediaries. Therefore, understanding how Defi works requires knowledge pertaining to three important topics: blockchain technology, Ethereum, and smart contracts.

Blockchain

Blockchain technology is the foundation for not only Defi but everything related to cryptocurrencies as well. In short, blockchains are digital ledgers that permanently record immutable data made out of publicly shared blocks with everyone.

Bitcoin, the first blockchain network, was launched in 2009 and is a game-changing idea because of security and scarcity.

Security

Blockchain networks like Bitcoin utilize the Proof of Work (PoW) consensus mechanism to execute transactions. PoW entails the employment of energy and hardware power by users known as miners to solve difficult mathematical problems in exchange for incentives earned by confirming blocks.

A block is a collection of signed transactions submitted by ordinary users who wish to send their money. Each transaction has a hash that verifies its ledger chronological sequence. As a result, each block has its hash linked to the preceding block's hash, creating a sequential chain of blocks.

It is almost difficult to attack Bitcoin since the whole ledger (a blockchain's transaction history) is spread in the form of copies across thousands of nodes. To create a new consensus and agree to a different version of the blockchain, a malevolent person would need to control more than 50% of the network's nodes (devices operated by miners).

Scarcity

Bitcoin is limited because there is a finite number of coins available. Unlike fiat currencies, it is impossible to manufacture and issue new coins indefinitely on the blockchain since the restriction is built into the cryptocurrency. Only 21 million Bitcoin will ever exist, and as more miners put coins onto the market, the circulating supply will steadily grow.

Scarcity enables Bitcoin to function as a store-of-value asset, which means it can be used as a haven or hedge in times of need, which is why investors refer to Bitcoin as "digital gold." When combined with excellent cryptographic security, scarcity makes Bitcoin one of the best-performing investment assets of all time.

Ethereum & Smart Contracts

Ethereum and Smart Contracts Ethereum is another cryptocurrency that adds to the usefulness of blockchain technology by using smart contracts, which are written in the Solidity programming language and used to build a rich dApp ecosystem with on-chain functionality other than payments.

Smart contracts, as previously said, are self-executing computer programs that operate autonomously and activate based on preset circumstances. Smart contracts provide significant advantages such as decentralization, security, and transparency, despite their slower execution speed when compared to centralized data systems.

Anyone can see and analyze the code of a smart contract to see whether it is malicious or not, which is a stark contrast to the banking industry. Furthermore, smart contracts do not take sides and only perform what they are instructed, ensuring that an Ethereum transaction will never take an unexpected turn.

Smart contracts are third-party mediators that handle transactions and agreements reached by at least two people. They eliminate the requirement for trust in an otherwise trustless system by allowing users to employ smart contracts instead of depending on the other party's good faith. They also let users avoid centralized middlemen like exchanges and banks, which would normally assist them with on-chain transactions.

To conclude, Ethereum may be seen as a smart contract-enabled version of Bitcoin, allowing it to execute computational logic and enable functionalities otherwise unavailable in first-generation blockchains.

Gas Fees

Users engage directly with smart contracts in Defi; thus, there are no gas fees. All of the goods and services are non-custodial, which means that assets may stay in the user's wallet rather than being deposited on the platform. A person may, for example, exchange tokens on Uniswap straight from his MetaMask.wallet. The disputed coins are never stored in Uniswap's native crypto wallets. The tokens are instead exchanged for other tokens in the exchange's smart contracts.

While the noncustodial feature increases the degree of decentralization in Defi, it comes at a high cost, which may discourage investors. A centralized exchange typically processes internal transactions to transfer assets, with no extra costs other than the trading fees. Because a DEX does not store the assets directly and requires the user to engage with smart contracts, all transactions are subject to Ethereum's gas fees.

How Ethereum Gas Power Transactions

All blockchain networks are supported by miners, a group of users who host nodes and confirm transactions. Blockchains must compensate miners with transaction fees to attract them and allow them to function in the first place.

On Ethereum, transaction costs are referred to as gas fees. Every conceivable smart contract transaction or activity, like as moving tokens, verifying balances, executing a smart contract function, and so on, consumes gas.

Another function of gas is that it establishes priority for various tasks. The greater the expense, the more difficult the job. As a result, gas acts as a limit, preventing the network from being overburdened by low-cost, basic operations.

When there aren't enough miners, and Ethereum sees a spike in activity, the blockchain encounters a phenomenon known as network congestion. Gas costs soar at that point, and the gas price for all transactions rises as well. Congestion on the network may persist for weeks, if not months, and the blockchain's status can only revert to normal if demand decreases. Fees may run from $40 to $100 per transaction, if not more, in certain instances. Because fees make for a major part of their transactions, investors who trade small sizes are naturally inclined to pause their Defi activity during this time.

How Decentralized Is Defi?

It's difficult to say how decentralized Defi is. For the purpose of simplicity, we shall divide decentralization into three categories: centralized, semi-decentralized, and entirely decentralized.

1. Centralized

- Features: Custodial, centralized price feeds, centralized interest rates, and centralized liquidity for margin calls.

- Examples include Celsius, Nexo, BlockFi, and Salt.

2. Decentralized to a degree (has one or more of these characteristics but not all)

- Features: Decentralized platform development/updates, decentralized interest rate determination, permissionless margin liquidity, permissionless initiation of margin calls, decentralized price feeds, noncustodial

- Examples include bZx, dYdX, MakerDAO, Compound.

3. Completely Decentralized

- Features: All the components are decentralized

- Examples include: No Defi protocol is completely decentralized yet.

The Defi Dashboard

A dashboard is a simple platform that centralizes all of your Defi activities. It is a great tool for seeing and tracking the location of your assets across various Defi protocols. The dashboard can categorize your assets into many categories, such as deposits, debt, and investments.

When you access your dashboard, you will typically be required to provide your Ethereum address (e.g.: 0x4Cdc86fa95Ec2704f0849825f1F8b077deeD8d39). You could also specify your Ethereum Name Service (ENS) domain. A human-readable Ethereum address that you can acquire for a set amount of time is known as an ENS domain. It's analogous to Internet domain names like www.coingecko.com, which then map to the server's IP address where CoinGecko is hosted.

There are various dashboards available on the market that can track your assets, like Frontier, InstaDApp, MyDeFi, and Zerion. To keep things simple, we'll look at DeFiSnap, one of the more well-known dashboards.

Step-By-Step Guide To Using Defisnap

Step 1:

Navigate to https://www.defisnap.io

Enter your ENS domain or Ethereum address.

I used defiportal.eth here, but I can also enter 0x358a6c0f7614c44b344381b0699e2397b1483252.

Step 2

You're on the dashboard!

You can view your wallet balance as well as any Defi deposits, debt, and investments.

2.   Tools to Utilize in DeFi

In this chapter of the guide, you will learn tips and tricks to; becoming your own bank, avoid paying capital gains tax, and how you can take money from your assets without selling it. While of course it sounds good I will also display the caveats involved with each method along with my opinion.

Borrow and Lending

Borrowing and lending in crypto can be very dangerous if you don't understand the mechanics.

In crypto there are two methods you can use to borrow funds. The first being through a centralized exchange like BlockFi or Celsius. The second way you can borrow funds is through a Decentralized exchange like compound or Aave.

Two ways to borrow crypto:

1. Through a centralized exchange

2. Through a decentralized exchange

Borrowing Through a Centralized Exchange

Borrowing though a crypto exchange is fairly different from taking a loan through a traditional bank. The concept is unique and gives everybody a chance to take a loan out. Now let me clarify that when you are borrowing in this type of method you are borrowing against yourself which benefits a person if they do not want to sell their assets. Now there are loans that don't require you to have any capital upfront.

So, if you have crypto in your account, you can use that crypto as collateral for a loan. You can use your crypto as collateral and withdraw USD, accessing your crypto value without selling your crypto.

Two types of loans:

1. Collateralized- exchanging your asset for a loan
2. Uncollateralized- A loan without any assets backing it

Why is not having to sell your crypto important? Well, if you believe that your investments will go up in price over time, you may not want to sell them before they reach that maturity. Also, you don't have to pay capital gains tax on that money since it is a loan.

In a traditional loan if you miss a payment, your credit score is impacted. There are no credit scores involved in a DeFi loan.

Instead, when you borrow from yourself there are two things that can happen. The first being you can simply pay back the loan in agreed upon terms. Now if you miss a payment, you are charged more in interest. The second thing that can happen is your asset that you Overcollateralized on can get liquidated.

Being liquidated can happen in two ways;

1. Not paying the loan back in agreed upon terms
2. 80% LTV

LTV stands for **Loan to Value**. So, if your loan reaches 80% the value of your asset than your asset will be liquidated.

In most cases you can only borrow 50% of your USD value in btc (Each exchange is different).

Example:

You decide that you want to borrow $1000 worth of your bitcoin. Meaning your bitcoin USD value must be at least $2000. So, to be liquidated your LTV has to be 80%.

LTV (%) = Loan Amount/Value of collateral

So, let's say hypothetically that the value of that $2000 drops to $1200 because the price of bitcoin falls, you would become liquidated. The equation would look as follows:

$$\frac{\text{Loan amount} \$1000}{\text{Value of Collateral} \$1200} \times 100 = 83.3\% \text{LTV}$$

In order to not become liquidated when your LTV goes above 80% you must pay down the loan amount. So, using the example above if the value of your collateral is $1200 you want to pay your loan amount down to $500 to keep that 50%LTV.

LTV levels:

50%- safe

65%- you'll begin to get warning messages by the broker

70%- you would begin getting margin calls from this point you would have 72 hours to pay down loan.

80%- automatic liquidation

Cryptocurrencies are very volatile, so you want to be very cautious and always monitor your LTV levels.

Lending Through a Centralized Exchange

This method is comparable to a savings account. I have seen platforms paying up to 9% in interest. Now it is variable, and you can check which platforms has the best rates with the link below.

Linkà https://loanscan.io/

We now understand how traditional banks truly work. Remember when you hold your money in a savings account, they do not lend it out, instead they balance their books with it so they can leverage more debt from the federal reserve.

The thought you had before about traditional banks lending your money out holds true in a centralized crypto exchange. In the beginning of the book, I promised I'd teach you how to become your own bank this isn't it. We are getting there this method just teaches you that you can utilize a smarter way of saving.

While both lending and borrow through an exchange sounds appetizing, I want to mention that you have to give custodian of your coins away. I have said it many times but, I am going to highlight it again **NOT YOUR KEYS NOT YOUR COINS!⚠** Using an exchange in any kind of way with crypto goes against the entire purpose of why crypto was invented. I am personally not a fan of this method and I do not use it, but while that is my opinion the facts are there, and the choice is yours. I want you to know so you can make an educational decision on how you handle your money. Read on and I will teach the methods I use.

Decentralized Lending and Borrow

Allows users to become lenders or borrowers in a completely decentralized way. Instead of giving your information to an exchange, DeFi protocols such as Aave and Compound run smart contracts on the Ethereum blockchain. These types of tokens operate by creating money markets. Users can choose which ever money market they want to lend their money to and start receiving interest right away (commonly known as yield farming). Now lending in this method works a lot different than lending through a CEX. Remember DEX's do not use order books they use AMM and the formula for AMM is $x*y=k$. So, when you lend to DEX's you lend token A (x) and Token B (y) which equals the amount of liquidity you are providing (k) as a constant. The interest you receive is not in dollars or in the pair you supplied, instead it is in the native token of the protocol you are lending in.

Example:

In this example we will use the liquidity pool LAZIO-BNB which is offering an APR of 138.5%, which sounds very attractive. How it works is you supply token A- LAZIO and token B-BNB which in return gives you interest in the native protocol which is Pancakes token CAKE. Now the cavate to this method is the effect of impermanent loss. Impermanent loss happens when the price ratio of the deposited tokens changes. Since the liquidity you provided is a constant if the price of the tokens you supply increases or decreases your liquidity pool is at a loss unless either the price reverts back, or you receive enough in fees to make up that loss. If you decide to withdraw the funds at a loss, then that loss becomes a permanent loss.

On the borrowing side borrowers choose to take collateralized loans out, flash loans or any other service that specific protocols offers. The interest that lenders receive and the interest that borrowers pay are determined by the overall ratio between supplied and borrowed tokens. The interest is calculated per Ethereum block (Ethereum block time usually 13 seconds), so interest rates fluctuate at a very fast rate.

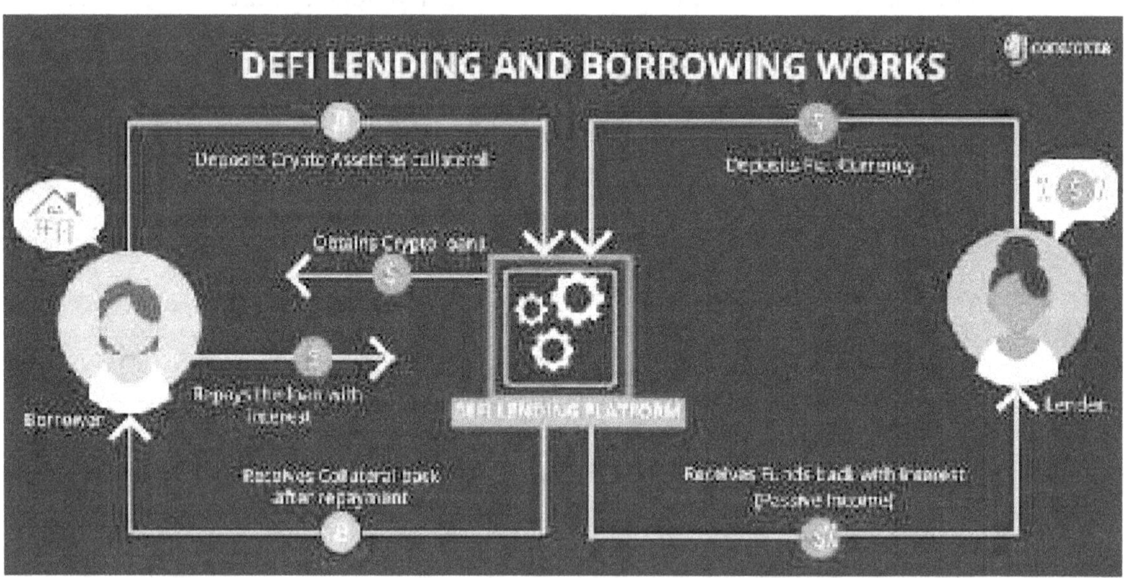

The liquidation process works the exact same as crypto exchanges use them. Some tokens have slightly different parameters for their LTV and liquidation levels. Below shows a chart on each protocol:

Liquidation stats for different protocols (with ETH as collateral)			
Protocol	MaterDAO	Compound	Aave
Minimum collateralization ratio	150%	133%	133%
Maximum loan-to-value	66.70%	75%	75%
Liquidation point (Min.coll.ratio)	<150%	<133%	<125
Liquidation point (LTV)	>66.70%	>75%	>80%
Liquidation factor	1	0.5	0.5
Liquidation penalty	13%	8%	5%

Most people borrow in a decentralized token to avoid paying taxes on their gains and not give up custodian to their coins.

The next tool mentioned is what I utilize to earn passive income. This protocol allows me to gain price appreciation and earn inflation from newly minted coins like Bitcoin miners do. It is the token that did a 1,000,000% gain in under two years. Sounds too good to be true? Go check the charts. It is an unbelievable financial instrument running on the block chain.

HEX Token

Hex is like a certificate of deposit (CD) that is run on the blockchain. Its game theory can be confusing but is superior and will shock you once you understand it. Hex is a token build on the Ethereum blockchain. Hex uses a staking consensus mechanism that allows anyone to stake their coins. When a person stakes their coins, they can lock them up to 15 years (I have stakes locked up for that long). When you lock your coins up, they burn off the market and you receive what's called T-shares or B-shares depending how much you lock and for how long. Those shares are your money printers, so every day at 8pm EST each T-share you have gives you on average 5.74 hex. That hex you receive is the newly minted inflation.

Example:

You lock your money up for 7 years and receive 15 T-shares and the price of hex is $1. Everyday you make 86.1 hex. Convert that to dollars every week your making $602.

15(T-shares) x 5.74 (Inflation)= 86.1 hex * 7 days * $1

 = $602 per week.

Now as time goes on the price of hex continues to rise so your money will begin to compound at a very rapid rate.

So, you receive additional hex everyday plus price appreciation when the price is up.

People who stake their money hold the price up and people who hold their bags liquid get diluted because the stakers are receiving all the inflation. The average stake length at the time of this writing is 5.74 years.

Anybody who stakes their coins and doesn't serve out half their stake time will get penalized and half that penalty will go to the origin address (OA) and the other half will go to the staker class.

The price of 1- T-share a year ago was .60 cents, today it is over $9,000! The T-share rate only goes up and to the rate which causes the hex price to only go up and to the right.

Hex is an amazing asset if you want to become your own bank! T-shares are money printers and get you paid every day.

Linkà Hex.com

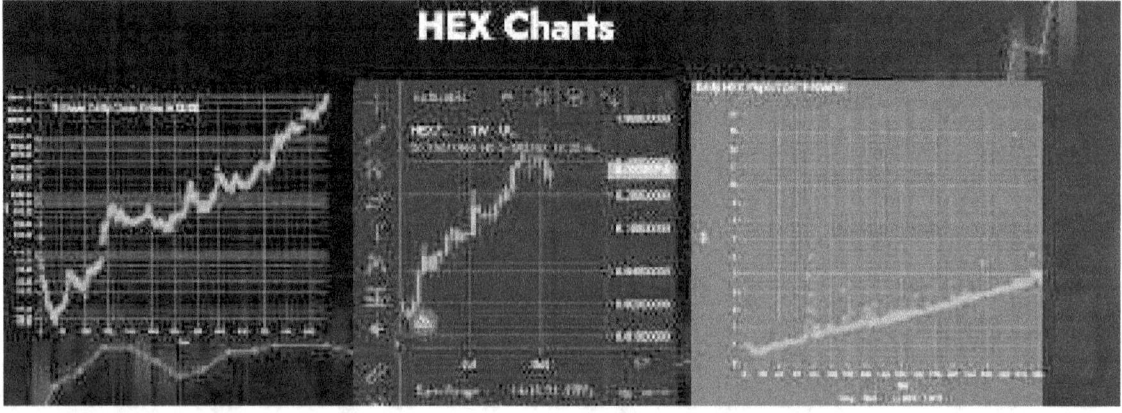

Up and to the right!

3. Decentralized Exchanges

Decentralized exchanges, also referred to as DEXs, are peer-to-peer markets where crypto investors conduct transactions without entrusting their assets to an intermediary. Such transactions are made possible via smart contracts, which are self-controlling contracts written in code.

DEXs were developed to eliminate the need for any authority to supervise and allow deals inside a given exchange. Peer-to-peer (P2P) cryptocurrency trading is possible on decentralized exchanges. Peer-to-peer refers to a cryptocurrency marketplace that connects buyers and sellers. They are often non-custodial, meaning that participants retain control over their wallet's private keys. Participants may access their cryptocurrency via a private key, which is a kind of sophisticated encryption. After authenticating into the decentralized exchange with their private key, participants may instantly see their cryptocurrency balances. They will not be needed to provide any personal details or addresses, which is ideal for those who value their privacy.

How DEXs Work

All trade induces a transaction cost in addition to the trading fee since DEXs are built on top of blockchain technology that allows smart contracts and where participants maintain custody of their assets. To use decentralized exchanges, traders engage with smart contracts on the blockchain network.

Automated market makers (AMM), Order books DEXs, and DEX aggregators are the primary forms of DEXs. All of them employ smart contracts to enable participants to trade freely with one another. The early DEXs utilized order books that were comparable to those used by centralized exchanges.

Automated Market Makers (AMMs)

An automated market maker (AMM) system based on smart contracts was developed to address the liquidity issue.

These AMMs use blockchain oracles, which are blockchain-supported services that offer data from exchanges and other networks to establish the price of traded assets. Rather than matching buy and sell orders, these DEXs' smart contracts employ liquidity pools, which are pre-funded pools of assets.

Other participants finance the pools, and they are then subject to the transaction fees charged by the system for implementing transactions on that pair. To earn income on their crypto assets, these liquidity providers must deposit an equal amount of all assets in the trading pair. A process referred to as liquidity mining. If they try to deposit more of an asset than another, the smart contract that runs the pool invalidates the transaction.

Traders can utilize liquidity pools to implement orders or get interest without needing permission or trust. Because the AMM concept has a disadvantage when there isn't sufficient liquidity, these exchanges are frequently rated based on the amount of cash held in their smart contracts, known as total value locked (TVL).

Order Book DEXs

Order books keep track of all open purchase and sell orders for certain asset pairs. Purchase orders show a trader's willingness to purchase or bid for an asset at a specified price, while sell orders show an investor's willingness to sell or ask for the item in question at a given price. The size of the order book and the market price on the exchange is determined by the gap between these values.

There are two forms of order book DEXs. They are on-chain order books and off-chain order books. Open order information is frequently held on-chain by DEXs that employ order books, while participants' money stays in their wallets. Investors on these exchanges could leverage their holdings by borrowing money from lenders on the site. Leveraged trading improves a trade's earning potential while equally increasing the danger of liquidation. It boosts the size of the position with borrowed money that must be returned even if the investors lose their stake.

On the other hand, DEX platforms that keep their order books off the blockchain simply execute orders on the blockchain to provide traders with the advantages of centralized exchanges. Exchanges can save money and time by using off-chain order books to ensure that deals are performed at the prices that participants want.

These exchanges equally enable participants to lend their cash to other investors to provide leveraged trading opportunities. Loaned money accrue interest with time and is protected by the exchange's liquidation process, which ensures that lenders are compensated even if investors lose theirs.

It's worth noting that order book DEXs frequently have liquidity difficulties. Traders generally adhere to centralized platforms as they are contending with centralized exchanges and pay extra expenses due to the fees needed to transact on-chain. While decentralized exchanges with off-chain order books decrease these expenses, the requirement to deposit cash in smart contracts introduces smart contract-related vulnerabilities.

DEX aggregators

To deal with liquidity issues, DEX aggregators employ a variety of protocols and methods. These platforms effectively pool liquidity from many decentralized exchanges to reduce slippage on big orders, reduce swap fees and token prices, and provide traders with a better price in the shortest amount of time.

DEX aggregators' other major aims are to protect participants from the price effect and reduce the chance of unsuccessful transactions. Certain DEX aggregators additionally leverage liquidity from centralized systems to give a better user experience, all while staying non-custodial through the usage of specialized centralized exchange integrations.

DYdX

Although dYdX is restricted basically as a trading platform, it is among the most sophisticated as an open, trustless, and non-custodial platform. Fundamental trading between three simple assets (ETH, DAI, and USDC), lending funds to earn interest, and major types of margin trading (isolated margin trading and cross margin trading) are presently available on the platform. These are basic instruments for a seasoned trader, but they represent a big step forward for the DeFi market.

dYdX closes deals on the blockchain network but employs an off-chain matching algorithm to provide the same implementation speeds as centralized exchanges while maintaining the security of non-custodial assets.

How it Works

Everybody engages in one "universal lending pool," rather than separate borrowers and lenders offering and receiving loan proposals. Every asset has its lending pool, which is handled by smart contracts, allowing for instant withdrawals, borrowing, and lending without necessarily waiting for matches or adequate money. The interest rates of any asset are determined by the interplay between borrowers and lenders–demand and supply.

Margin Trading

dYdX enables margin trading in conjunction with spot trading (changing one digital token to another), allowing cryptocurrency investors to perform more complex trading methods.

Margin trading, equally referred to as leveraged trading, enables traders to take greater holdings by borrowing money from a third party. Not only does this enable expert traders to increase their trading earnings (and losses!), but it equally allows regular traders to take greater holdings with a smaller amount of initial cash.

Example:

If you're optimistic about Ethereum, you might use a $1,000 initial margin to enter a 5x leveraged trade on ETH/USDC. In that situation, you'd have $5,000 worth of ETH/USDC exposure. If the price increased by 10%, the position would be increased by $500 (rather than just $100), giving you a 50% return on your investment if you closed it out at that time.

If the bullish conviction is incorrect and the price of ETH falls by $10 against USDC, the worth of the $1000 5x leveraged position will be reduced to $500. A 50% drop in value.

All you have to do to begin trading on dYdX is link your Ethereum wallet. The Trust Wallet in-app DApp Browser is the easiest method to achieve this on mobile. You may also use Wallet-Connect to access the web-supported edition of dYdX.

Traders can also use margin trading to short assets they anticipate will fail. Short selling an asset entails borrowing it to sell it and then purchasing it back later (ideally at a lower price) to benefit whenever the asset's value declines.

If Ethereum's bearish anticipates the cryptocurrency's price will fall in the following days, they may utilize dYdX to short ETH against USDC or DAI (with up to 5x leverage).

How to Make Money with dYdX

If you've ever searched through aggregators of DeFi loan rates, you've probably come across dYdX. Because the platform is decentralized, participants may borrow and lend Ethereum-supported assets.

dYdX makes it easier to earn interest on digital assets than any other DeFi protocol. It's straightforward. You will begin to receive interest immediately after you deposit cash into the platform on the 'Balances' tab. That's all there is to it! And every minute that your dollars are stored in the platform, you will receive interest.

Borrowing (mainly margin traders) on the platform pays interest on stored assets. Because dYdX allows only collateral-based borrowing, if borrowers fail to repay or their collateral value falls below a set limit, their collateral is instantly liquidated to safeguard lenders.

dYdX has reproduced the famous cryptocurrency derivatives offering from prominent centralized exchanges like Bitfinex and BitMEX in a safe, transparent, and trustless manner, rendering it better than its centralized counterparts in many respects.

Uniswap

Uniswap is an Ethereum platform for trading ERC20 tokens. Uniswap, unlike other exchanges, is meant to be a public good—a means for the public to trade tokens without paying platform fees or dealing with intermediaries. Uniswap also utilizes basic arithmetic and pools of tokens and ETH to accomplish the same function as conventional exchanges that connect buyers and sellers to establish prices and conduct transactions.

How It Work

In comparison to centralized exchanges, the Uniswap platform takes a unique approach. Its open-source program is based on the Ethereum network, and it enables participants to trade ERC-20 tokens without the involvement of a third party. This can assist in decreasing expenses while also resolving certain tricky censorship concerns.

Without the use of an order book, liquidity providers play a critical role in making things happen. Anybody can participate in these liquidity pools by contributing the equal value of two tokens, like ETH and stablecoins like USDT or DAI. They'll earn liquidity pool tokens in return, which they may spend on other decentralized applications. This equally assures that they will be able to receive their donation at any moment.

When participants conduct a swap using a trading pair, they are charged transaction fees, with a part of this going to the liquidity provider according to the pool tokens they possess.

Uniswap pools are based on the equation "$x * y = k.*$."

Here, x might be ETH, y could be USDT, and k could be the result of multiplying x and y to find the pool's total liquidity. Constant product market makers — smart contracts that store liquidity pools — assume that k must always be fixed.

Assume that somebody buys ETH in exchange for USDT via a liquidity pool. As a result of this trade, there will be less ETH in the liquidity pool and more USDT.

Somebody who buys ETH from a liquidity pool in return for USDT will adjust the balance between the assets in this transaction pair, raising the price of ETH while lowering the price of USDT. In bigger liquidity pools, this slippage is typically less evident.

Uniswap's major benefits are its ease of use compared to other DEXs and the fact that traders are no longer accountable for supplying liquidity.

How Uniswap Tokens are Created

The donor gets a "pool token," which is also an ERC20 token, anytime fresh ETH/ERC20 tokens are given to a Uniswap liquidity pool.

When money is placed into the pool, pool tokens are produced, and like an ERC20 token, they may be freely traded, transferred, and utilized in other Dapps. The pool tokens are burnt or destroyed when money is recovered. Every pool token reflects a participant's portion of the pool's overall assets as well as their portion of the pool's 0.3 percent transaction fee.

How to Make Your First Uniswap Trade

You may buy ether (ETH) and any of the hundreds of ERC20 tokens offered by the platform using Uniswap.

To do so, you'll need enough ETH in your account to cover any transaction costs and something to exchange for the ERC20 token you desire. This may be ETH or another ERC20 token. If you want to trade USD Coin (USDC) for UNI, for instance, you'll require USDC in the wallet as well as enough ether to pay the trading fee.

We'll go through how to buy some UNI tokens with ETH and perform your first transaction on Uniswap.

- Step 1: Go to the Uniswap exchange site.

Select the 'Connect to a wallet' option in the top right corner, then log in with the wallet you want to transact with. A MetaMask, WalletConnect, Coinbase Wallet, Fortmatic, or Portis Wallet may be used.

We'll use a MetaMask wallet to log in for this explanation.

- Step 2: The transaction page will display once you've logged in.

Choose the token you like to swap for the other token you want in the top area. You may go with ETH. Look for the token you want to buy in the bottom area, or choose it from the drop-down option, in this instance UNI.

- Step 3: You're finally set to place your order.

You may enter a number in the top area to indicate what you like to spend or a number in the bottom area to indicate what you want to purchase.

Let's assume we acquire 0.1 ETH worth of UNI tokens in our illustration.

- Step 4: At the bottom of the order menu, you'll find an estimate of what you'll get.

Hit the 'Swap' option when you're satisfied with the results. The wallet click would then ask you to authorize the transaction and, if necessary, change the fees to a level that is most convenient for you.

Approve the transaction once you're set, and it'll be executed. The tokens will display in the ERC20 wallet after this is completed.

- Next Steps

There are many choices for advanced users after you've made your first transaction on Uniswap. Because Uniswap is an open smart contract platform, a variety of front-end user interfaces have already been developed. InstaDApp, for instance, enables you to deposit money into Uniswap pools without utilizing the regular Uniswap user interface.

Participants can add funds to Uniswap pools using only ETH rather than ETH and another token utilizing interfaces like Zapper.fi. Easy, one-click options for acquiring pool tokens in conjunction with bZx token schemes are available through the interface.

Balancer

Balancer is a decentralized exchange that uses an automated market maker (AMM) and liquidity pools. It is based on the Ethereum network. It allows participants to trade cryptos and receive interest on their unused crypto holdings.

Balancer participants can trade ERC-20 assets without depending on a centralized body by using liquidity pools. They may also offer liquidity in exchange for a portion of the trading fees. Balancer distinguishes itself from the competition by allowing customers to build their private liquidity pools or pools with more than two cryptos. Balancer provides several incentives to enhance liquidity on the Balancer Protocol in the long run.

Balancer token (BAL)

Balancer (BAL) is the Balancer protocol's native governance token. BAL token owners can vote on the protocol's growth. Although the network does not currently have a defined governance structure, token owners can vote on layer two solutions, the installation of Balancer on blockchains other than Ethereum, and fee adjustments at the protocol level.

How it Works

The Balancer exchange is an automated market maker (AMM), which implies transactions are settled without traditional order books. Balancer pools that are liquidity pools made up of 2 to 8 cryptos are used instead. These offer the liquidity that investors want. The AMM utilizes the percentage of tokens inside a liquidity pool to establish exchange rates. Smart contracts are used to accomplish exchanges.

Whenever a new Balancer pool is formed, the developer determines the token ratio in the pool. For example, if a pool contains Tether, Ether, and wBTC, the ratios might be adjusted to 25 percent, 25 percent, and 50 percent, respectively. When compared to Tether and Ether, there would be twice the amount of wBTC.

When a trader utilizes a liquidity pool to execute a transaction, the liquidity pool is rebalanced. Any imbalances in the pool might provide traders with arbitrage possibilities. The arbitrage trader makes money by taking advantage of the pool's imbalance compared to the actual-world market exchange rate. This arbitrage mechanism constantly rebalances the liquidity pool. However, fees are still collected from liquidity providers and individuals who formed the liquidity pool.

Balancer Pools

To accommodate varied risk appetites, Balancer provides two forms of pools: public pools and private pools. By contributing digital assets to public pools, anybody may offer liquidity to Balancer. These pools' settings are established before they go live and cannot be altered, even by the pool's creators. Stockholders that want to earn fees from their holdings might consider joining a public pool.

Private liquidity pools are those in which only the creator can add or remove assets. The developer also adjusted other pool criteria, such as allowed assets, fees, and weightings.

How to trade on Balancer

A participant will need access to cryptos through a Web 3.0 digital wallet like MetaMask before transacting on the Balancer platform. MetaMask is a browser plugin that serves as a link between the digital asset holdings and decentralized apps like Balancer.

To trade on Balancer, follow these steps:

- Balancer. Log onto the Balancer platform.
- Link your wallet. Link your Web 3.0 digital wallet, such as MetaMask
- Decide on a crypto. Select the crypto you want to sell or purchase from the dropdown set of possible tokens. You may accomplish this by entering the token's name, address, or symbol.
- Fill in the amount. Once you've made your choice, you'll need to input the quantity of crypto you want to trade. After filtering across relevant pools carrying the tokens required, Balancer will offer you the best potential price as you start to input the "token to sell" amount.
- Confirm. On your MetaMask or Web 3.0 digital wallet, click "Swap" and complete the transaction. The crypto sold will be withdrawn from the digital wallet when the transaction is completed on the Ethereum network, and the crypto acquired will be added.

4. Understanding Decentralization Myths

The people who plagiarize stuff on the internet, gaining control of all the networks and tools, put forward on their own the minor details of the problem that are included in the website that they plunder. Even though their viewpoint assures more but creates the following of a growing number of opponents. As people were made aware of Nakamoto's plans, splinter groups resembling an anemone were laid by Nakamoto, which resulted in the mass spread of cryptocurrencies & blockchains everywhere. It would have been an impeccable camouflage (the 2014 ICO Boom) for the attempt of the group at a coup on the United States, but failed when the boon of the industry was doubted as treachery by the US and Cicada stayed legally latent.

Even though I am not aware of the true initiative of Cicada but what I do know is that Cicada and Henrici are inclined to question in contradiction the ways of peace established. Similarly, Nakamoto questioned against the established ways of finance. With Nakamoto's paper began the Decentralized myth in cryptocurrency which meant that the government controlling the worth of value wouldn't be good. Like stocks, the governmental regulations do not determine the value of Bitcoin but instead, it gets its value from the values of its enterprise.

Nakamoto, whose identity nobody knows, through his name into the woodworks of an enterprise. Hypothetically an enterprise talking to a government. In order to control law enforcement high crime subsidies, in 2005 the United States was on the outlook for financial services. President Bush was counseled by his advisors to take notice of the usefulness of the storage of the value Bitcoin possessed, but it was a small-scale company and hence it didn't fit the desires of the American public.

The Homeland Security Act's Byrne Justice Assistance Grant was the winner of the competition for law enforcement. Robert Byrne of VA who was an ambulance chaser started this and it has been the hole in the bowl leaking America's funding. The first payment was made by the grant in 2006 with $6 billion being paid to the 17 states with peaking crime rates. The following year our Treasury secretary and a few of his pals start price-fixing credit ratings for promissory notes.

His action is conceivable only if the Nakamoto paper belittles governments and the funding of high crime states for having high crime are all about money, which they were. This action ended up collapsing three industries i.e., Banking, Housing, and Automobiles. Successively, there was a scarcity of jobs in not only America but the world too.

Satoshi Nakamoto went underground and was never heard from again. Further calamity was caused in America as the money used to subsidize law enforcement high-crime grants could not be used to fortify banks, so naturally, America had to ask for money. The promoting businesses, who were held accountable for this catastrophe received money, which resulted in businesses coming up and discovering new ways to fund the catastrophe (Oil Surplus) to accept bailout similar to the promoting businesses. All those who actually contributed to this catastrophe would come across a calamity from their own business plans but Bitcoin would prove to be a savior for a few.

2008 has Bitcoin catch traction with the introduction of Reddit and 4Chan. This turned Bitcoin into a cryptocurrency used to gamble, buy chat room game collectibles, buy NFTs, which was soon followed with it being assumed "real-world" value with the initial "transaction" when for 10,000 Bitcoin, two large Pizzas were bought from Papa Johns. Which was followed by the big leagues as the designer NFTs and the Pizza story turned into a bizarre art and costly electronics out of China. The Casinos of the Chinese Islands were told that they needed to be a part of the act, so they built an online casino that only accepted Bitcoin

At present, Decentralized Autonomous Organization (DAO) has the ownership of numerous cryptocurrencies of their own, not Bitcoin. Even though loyalty is centralized, Bitcoin is still used at the Casinos for loyalty tokens. Their point is that they are their own business and it didn't take long to understand that, nor did it matter.

The significant concept of the decentralized myth is Loyalty. Initially sold as a loyalty token Bitcoin became the target of attempted plagiarism which ended up stealing a 99% share of the market awareness. It was sheer luck that the remaining 1% turned into such a strong network of finance which was equivalent in wealth to the economy of Venezuela, the 6th largest economy in the world. The aggressive attempt certainly had a windfall, and market analysis anticipates regulation to end the oppression and create a strategy for mass adoption.

Bitcoin is not Satoshi Nakamoto as a BX in Thailand, as proved by regulatory issues. Policies like AML/KYC, introduced by governments to capture Satoshi Nakamoto were utilized Bitcoin's home exchange. Additionally, determining projects such as Civic by Roger, Ver, or Pavo by IBM, within cryptocurrency seek to do business with governments. Laws of all the top 10 nations with well-developed economies permit the fair trade of cryptocurrency under-regulated measures which is the description of regulated by a central bank.

The dominant philosophy of the decentralized myth that started with the publishing of the Satoshi Nakamoto paper was to upkeep misconduct by derestricting currency. The weakness was that the governments have money as well.

Though the decentralized myth did give us some positive outcomes. Firstly, the elucidation of how transaction processing was crowdsourced by Bitcoin through publicly outsourcing mining algorithms procreated the concept of crowdsourcing. Crowd-funding was acclaimed as a harmless method of finance while the Initial Coin Offerings (ICOs) were thought of as evil.

$200 million was gathered by the ICO market in the year 2017, which was its peak time. But unfortunately, it also brought a lot of fraud and scams. Out of all the ICOs that collected the money barely half of them started doing business. Since it was free money, there were no accountabilities if you didn't raise enough. It wasn't expected for the cryptocurrency to go any farther than video games and the internet unless it had a blockchain.

2018 was the revolutionary year because this was the time when every project was unexpectedly in need of a real-world application. Cryptocurrency and Bitcoin was no longer just a token for video games but instead, it was an entire financial instrument. The products related to agriculture presently had validation of freshness and were followed by augmented reality games and artificial intelligence.

2019 witnessed the dirty business of manipulation and deregulation. Manipulation is all about setting up others just so your chances are better. In cryptocurrency, manipulation was all about the fights regarding the decentralized myth with the biggest question being about mass adoption. "Bitcoin Purists" were in favor of upholding the instability of the currency to keep the hedging long, while finance-minded organizations were in favor of stabilizing the currency. The gamers and coders and had the power to diverge the steadiness and ensure volatility. The BCC fork was more of an inspiration to Congress for needing a diverse structure for the tax for a few businesses. So, we can say that deregulation of the cryptocurrency created more users in a way. This is something that would flame the arguments that shaped the modern cryptocurrency exchange.

Now according to the AML/KYC policies, the US has to tax structures for Bitcoin businesses who envisioned the 'deregulation' as the position the industry would stand on going into the next decade, and over 34,000 crypto exchanges. To the public eye, the word decentralized has developed into an occurrence that is greater than cryptocurrency... crowdsourcing.

But crowdsourcing is only one of the concepts of decentralization. The deleterious aspect that was discovered by the myth has both good and bad consequences. On one hand, crime is being lured into the industry. Cryptocurrency is seen by many as a way out of an undesirable lifecycle, while according to those in finance who are wise, the myth is drafting criminals for an overthrow plot, which is similar to the chance taken by Pro-Trump demonstrators when attacking the capital.

The only real danger posed by the myth was that it was supposed to target governments so that companies like General Motors could protest against the government until being given a bailout. All in all, decentralization took on more significance than the threat posed on the world by Lee Iacocca. Lee Iacocca wanted to build every car driven and own every business. And he would go to any limits to achieve his aim and nothing would stop him to accomplish what he wished for and wanted, not even a forged racial identity.

Blockchain is not a threat:

Media and pundits alike are inspired by cryptocurrencies and their fundamental technology – the blockchain.

Since the technological setup of the blockchain is complex and would confuse not only the average reader but the crypto-lovers too, they might not be acquainted with the financial terminology and payment infrastructure.

Due to this unfamiliarity, many persistent myths have been born that have reinforced most blockchain discussions. Most of these myths are either wrong or too one-dimensional and, thus they cloud the aptitude of decision-makers to make judgments and ability to reach conclusions.

There are three tangled assumptions that jointly fuel the argument regarding blockchain technology breaking banks.

Myth 1: "Open blockchains rather than closed will power tomorrow's economy"

The main reason for the spread of blockchain technology was the excitement and enthusiasm of people about getting rid of banks. When Bitcoin was created in 2008, due to the financial crisis the following of blockchain technology grew rapidly. A solution to the financial system run by big financers was presented in the form of the technical arrangement of Bitcoin and its decentralized nature it has. Although it was later seen that decentralization was not mandatory for a blockchain.

There are two general major blockchain setups:

- Centralized or "closed"
- Decentralized or "open"

Every blockchain system has a system of multiple nodes to upkeep a ledger instead of having a middleman. This shows that the blockchain system is distributed. In decentralized ("open") no node is advantaged over the others by the algorithm. On the contrary, in centralized ("closed") chains some nodes are given more weightage than others.

In a decentralized blockchain- like Bitcoin, where everybody can participate in verifying transactions and each node carries the same weight.

Though, there is not always a precise discrepancy. In Ripple, one out of the three major crypto coins, the degree of centralization is still debated and disputed upon within the industry. The case with it as a blockchain is similar, the transactions that are recorded are not piled up as blocks, instead, they look like a large ledger. So the question arises, why does this distinction matter?

There are many limitations to the original, decentralized model. Some of these include the un-maintainable energy-consumption, the unapproachable necessary scale, the usability a pain, and regulation a thing to be circumvented by design, financial transactions taking far too long, more-over the currency problems faced by crypto-coins and this can lead us to understand the cynicism of many officials. All these weaknesses and limitations could have been eliminated in the central-ized blockchains as the majority of the financial institutions regard it as the model of choice.

Despite all this why is the hype around the open blockchain? This technological disagreement is indicative of a deep ideological split at the center of the blockchain debate. On one side, there are officials of the banking and payments world, whereas on the other side what we see is an unusual coalition of crypto-evangelists, anarcho-libertarians, entrepreneurs, and fraudsters who are set for the commotion. The concluding group characterizes the founders and early adopters of the blockchain and still carries substantial weight in determining public debate about it. What they see in the blockchain is the means to bring down any kind of trusted institution which according to them is only possible with truly decentralized applications.

Myth 2: "With the success of the blockchain comes the downfall of banks"

Bearing in mind the background of primary investors of crypto, it is possibly conventional that banks are announced to be the first targets of the blockchain.

As stated, however, the model with at least some kind of centralization will be the winning mod-el. This already cries out for a dealer of trust, implying that banks will be part of the equation. And even if the algorithm is completely decentralized there will still be some institutions that would need to handle data and rights to access pre or post a transaction. Bitcoins also have such institutions which are exchanges, you can trade, buy or sell bitcoin on these exchanges. Even bit-coins need institutions such as exchanges where you can buy and sell them.

Just a small part of the banks' value chain is comprised of payments. Even if cryptocurrencies succeeded to displace banks from moving value, what they wouldn't be able to do is replace them in providing everlasting and steady storage of value. Neither could the supplying of fi-nances work devoid of financial institutions. Blockchains do not break into the banks, but the banks can break into markets so they can accept the digital standard.

Myth 3: "FinTechs are the banks' main challenge"

This third myth impeccably merges in with the first two. Decentralization, as opposed to the very nature of banks, lays the foundation for their fall and therefore, there also needs to be an immac-ulate challenger to push them from their throne.

The young and nimble FinTechs are responsible for this role. They start anew and can dedicate their entire energy to new products. Dynamic FinTechs can easily follow along any direction that the market takes. It has already happened to retail and hardware-manufacturing, and now it is also happening to finance?

The real reason why these examples are so noticeable is that they are the exclusion rather than the rule. Studies show that an industry structure is missed up not only due to greenfield competition, but the majority of the time it is due to incumbents or by market recruits prevailing in other industries. As a rule, new applicants lack the scale, financial muscle, and brand awareness. Typically, it takes longer to build those up than to guide mandatory supertankers into the winning direction.

Paypal is an example that is frequently mentioned when showing that banking is not immune to modernization. Dissimilar from Visa or Mastercard, it is not a result of banking collaboration, nevertheless, it has hitherto become the chief online payment system in North America. It comprises over 354 billion USD in payment volume internationally. The amount of active user accounts on Paypal has surpassed 200 million. But Paypal surrounds itself around the currently existing system. It does not succeed in credit cards or bank accounts but instead supplements them. Blockchain start-ups are an entirely different tale. Banks have realized long ago that the technology will aid them in saving a lot of money in the back-end. Innumerable initiatives, attainments, and blockchain labs are evidence of this. They will not be caught slumbering again.

And finally, one critical question rests: Do FinTechs really want to relocate the existing incumbents? Most mission statements definitely read as if this is the goal, yet in a study, 75.5% of all FinTechs announce that partnering with a recognized firm is their main goal. An intention might be that now the majority of the start-up blockchains are driven by obligatory investment like Veem took $25 million from cooperation run by Goldman Sachs.

The perseverance of these three myths definitely has sustained the interest in blockchain technology. These myths are unpretentious, speak to an engaged target group, and can be supported with carefully selected attention-grabbing examples. Believing them gullibly might end up costing you actual money – regardless of the fact if you are bearing in mind buying a crypto-coin or as a corporate decision-maker you anticipate financing original infrastructure.

Due to its mass of mechanisms and the resulting fuzziness, even more, fallacies surround blockchain technology. To devise a longstanding plan for blockchain that will not be directed by the latest news items, it is obligatory to clear those up.

5.   How to enter DeFi?

In order to get into DeFi investments, first we need to know some tools where to buy cryptocurrencies. These are the three main ones, let's know their advantages and disadvantages.

Binance

If you don't have an account yet, sign up from the following affiliate link and you'll enjoy 10% off **trading** fees for life:

https://www.binance.com/es/register?ref=QR0YPYFC

This is a platform for exchanging cryptocurrencies, is one of the most users in the world. it was launched in July 2017. It has an ICO to finance the development of the Exchange. This allows the platform not to depend on venture capital companies, being funded by the community.

Binance launched its ICO on July 3 and put up for sale 100 million ERC20 tokens called BNB (Binance Coin). It lasted just 3 minutes and managed to raise $15 million. 11 days after launching the ICO the Exchange was already available.

There were many registered users after the launch, it generated some access problems due to the large volume of users. Today it is valued at more than two billion dollars.

If we look at the Binance menu we find a series of options for each of its tasks:

- Exchange: to exchange cryptocurrencies, where real-time analysis of the market will appear.
- Academy: cryptocurrency education. Courses, tutorials and more on the subject.
- BCF: is a **blockchain** charitable foundation. Information about the company's charities and donations.
- Info: has information about cryptocurrencies, such as exchange rates, traded volumes and costs.
- Labs: is an incubator for outstanding **blockchain** projects. This is where the company's team that will develop **blockchain** solutions is located.
- Launch pad: is a platform for users to launch their own tokens.
- Research: has information about the company, about mission, tasks and who they are.
- Trust wallet: is an official cryptocurrency wallet.

It also has another series of folding menus on the upper right side. There a number of options appear:

- Funds: deposits, withdrawals, balances, withdrawal and deposit histories, and credit card purchases.
- Order management: you have open orders, order history and transaction history.
- Careers: application for studies with the academy.
- Support: information on common problems with users and solutions.
- News: recent publications in the press about the company and other related topics.

After seeing all this, let's look at the advantages and disadvantages of Binance.

Advantages

- You can open an account for free.
- You can choose the language in which you want to operate it.
- It is capable of processing one million transactions per second.
- Their fees are low for transactions and withdrawals.
- It has a community rewards program.

- There is security, and confidence. _
- Optional Visa card. _

Disadvantages

- At the beginning the handling can be complicated. _
- It has a support that could be tedious. _
- You have to go through KYC (Know Your Customer) registration._

Although it may have some disadvantages, when it comes to using it and knowing it, it is one of the best options and therefore one of the most used in the world.

Bit2Me

If you don't have an account yet, sign up from the following affiliate link and they will give you 5 euros if your first purchase is 100 euros or more:

https://bit2me.com/es/registro?r=GVT-J5S-DE3

Founded in 2014, it specializes in financial technology. It has a great knowledge in **blockchain** technology and cryptocurrencies, helping individuals, **exchanges**, mining **pools**, issuing tokens, investment funds, governments and institutions, trading and managing different digital assets in an optimal way.

It serves as a gateway to frictionless markets, rendering the traditional financial system obsolete. It was created with the vision of transparency and open and efficient financial systems. It supports many initiatives in the DeFi system, interacting with protocols, providing liquidity and participating in networks that encompass decentralized lending, trading and other financial applications.

The entire systems are developed internally by its operators and considers both a technological and commercial enterprise, creating products, processes and tools to change the world, with the goal of enabling frictionless, fair and transparent markets.

Among its functions we can find:

- Cryptocurrency wallet. _
- It has a trading platform. _
- Bit2me Pay._
- Crypto payments can be accepted in the business. _
- It has secure cryptocurrency custody. _
- Tikebit. _
- MasterCard to pay some cryptocurrencies. _
- Exclusive services for clients. _

Bit2Me released its own token called B2M. It's not in all countries yet, you can only use the platform if you reside in: Austria, Belgium, Bulgaria, Croatia, Cyprus, Czech Republic, Denmark, Estonia, Finland, France, Germany, Greece, Hungary, Ireland, Italy, Latvia, Lithuania, Luxembourg, Malta, Netherlands, Poland, Portugal, Romania, Slovakia, Slovenia, Spain, Sweden, UK. Argentina, Bolivia, Brazil, Chile, Colombia, Costa Rica, Dominican Republic, El Salvador, Mexico, Panama, Puerto Rico, Peru and Uruguay. The list is constantly growing so it is a good idea to check if it is already available in any other country you are interested in.

You have to create an account, before trading you have to go through a data validation process. It is a process that you achieve quickly. To be able to use it you need to have set up the profile well, filling in all the data and attaching your ID. It is an important step in this kind of platform.

There are those who do not trust this step, but the truth is that these operations are banking and it is necessary that you have your information here. If you become a millionaire, you can put on a face and then pay taxes like a good citizen. Another feature is that you have recently incorporated in Bit2Me Trade, for people who are new to the world of **trading** or for professionals.

It's not just for buying cryptocurrencies though. It is a team of people who provide knowledge and value to the community. This world is very wide and needs people to clarify all the information. They have their project called Academy, where they provide a lot of valuable information. It is a reliable exchange, although as confident as they are you should not trust your assets to any **exchange**, the good thing is that they share the same opinion. If you invest a lot to save and leave it in an external **wallet**, you should not have the money in the **blockchain**.

The point is to use it to buy with the affiliate link, remember that only for this you will be earning five euros when you make a purchase of one hundred. Then you can decide what to do with the cryptoassets, whether to keep them in the Exchange (which will soon offer **staking** options like the other two **exchanges** we see in this book) or send them to interact with some protocol.

Advantages

- Those responsible have faces and names. There is transparency, with a physical office, and there are many **exchanges** that do not. _
- They have customer service in Spanish. It is of high quality or at least they try. They even have a phone number. _
- They are available 24 hours a day, every day of the year. _
- There is a lot of information on their blog, they have tutorials and guides. _
- They have their own wallet. _
- They have a very active YouTube channel with interesting videos for you to learn more. _
- They currently have relevant people in their team. _

Disadvantages

- They are demanding in the verification process. _
- You can't find all the cryptocurrencies on the market to buy, but you can find the most important ones. _
- If you are going to make large investments, commissions may be very high. _

Coinbase

If you sign up for an account after clicking on the following affiliate link and if you buy or sell more than $100 in the first 180 days, you will receive $10 or the equivalent in another currency for free:

https://www.coinbase.com/join/blzque_ou

It is a great platform that offers you many advantages. Among them, you can see the graphs with the evolution of prices, you can know how the value of the cryptocurrencies you have goes up or down. Let's analyze this platform in detail.

It acts as a digital **wallet**, which means that you can use it to store your cryptocurrencies in a unified place. Think of it like your bank's app, where you can see the amount of cryptocurrencies you have and the value with their evolution. Also, each wallet will also have a unique address with which others can send cryptocurrencies to it, allowing you to receive or make payments with them without having to go through other services.

On the other hand, it is also a trading service, which is known as a cryptocurrency exchange. Here you can link your credit card and make use of the money to buy various cryptos.

With this, you have a service whose operation is very similar to others such as PayPal (something that Binance and Bit2Me do not yet allow) or your bank's app. You can manage them as if it were a stock market app, but instead of speculating on the market, you can do it with the cryptocurrency market.

The company is based in San Francisco, California, was founded in 2012 by Brian Armstrong and Fred Ehrsam. BBVA has been one of the major investors. It has more than 30 million users.

Coinbase charges you commissions when you buy or sell cryptocurrencies, when buying you have a commission of 1.49%, and when selling to convert them into fiat money, the commission is 1%. What it does not have is commission on transfers of assets to other virtual wallets.

To register is very easy, you just need to be of legal age, give the service the name, surname, email and password, you can make use in the account. Then you link another payment method that can be a PayPal account, bank, credit or debit card.

Coinbase can be used on mobile or on the website. You can see the fiat money value of your investments, the evolution of the main cryptos and decide which ones you want to be shown to you, seeing a summary of the outstanding news of the sector. There is a button called Trade, where you can buy, sell or convert cryptocurrencies. In any of the cases before accepting the operation will always appear the commission you have to pay so that everything is clear to you.

You will also see a bar with options like Portfolio, where you can know the status of the assets, seeing the money you have in the various cryptos and the evolution. In Coinbase the information also appears on the home page, and is deliberately in Portfolio.

You also find the Pricing section, where you can see the current status of the assets that allows you to manage Coinbase, both what you have bought and what you haven't bought. It will tell you the current state of the market in general, the value of the assets in real time, how much you have gone up or down with respect to the value of each asset in the last 24 hours.

You also have the settings section where you can add payment methods or make invitations to earn euro balance by getting others to sign up. You can set your local currency or purchase limits, which can be set to an amount of money per day in the steps or to spend without control what you want. You can set a PIN to protect the application, notifications, privacy or email.

Advantages

- It is the safest and simplest way to exchange real money for cryptocurrencies. _
- It offers a variety of withdrawal and deposit options. _
- All deposits are insured. _
- It has a multi-signature security level. _
- It has an affiliate program where you can earn 10 euros for every 100 euros invested by your referrals. _

Disadvantages

Here are the negative points you might want to consider:

- Private keys for cryptocurrencies are for the exclusive use of Coinbase, nobody knows them... not even you. _

- The account is constantly monitored for illegalities, if the algorithm detects any irregularities, Coinbase may close your account. _

All platforms are a great option

Although all three platforms studied have their disadvantages, they also have advantages, so all of them are an option for you to trade, all depending on your needs.

Although Binance and Coinbase have financial products that are more or less decentralized compared to what Bit2Me has, these **blockchain** based products allow you to trade and acquire and send them to your Metamask wallet and access the protocols.

Binance and Coinbase have always had a duel for which one is the best, this can be found in many forums around the internet. Both platforms differ in the type of cryptos they accept on the platforms. While the former has a wider portfolio, the latter is more exclusive. You have to look at the usability, since to have a good experience you need to find a platform that allows you to manage investments in a practical way.

Coinbase has some good opinions about its interface, which is very intuitive, compared to Binance which can be a bit overwhelming at first. The former can provide a more straightforward cryptocurrency trading and investment process.

About security, is it safe to leave assets on Binance? Yes, it supports users with two-factor authentication offered by Google Authenticator. It allows transactions and data modifications by entering the password and validating the access code sent by the mobile phone.

Coinbase is no slouch when it comes to security either, every action you take has its own insurance policy. There are funds in external **wallet**, avoiding hacks. So which one is better depends on the strategies you have in trading.

Binance is an attractive option for those who want to trade cryptos at reasonable rates, because in addition to having a lot of options, the commissions are the lowest, although as I said before, it can be complex to use. Although on mobile phone it has a version called Lite that you can enable or disable and make quick trades are so many buttons or menus.

Wallet

When you buy cryptocurrencies you must have a place to keep them and guard them. You must take care of them, just like when you withdraw money from the ATM. That is why it is important that you have a wallet or wallet and know the types, uses and risks of each one.

Deciding which wallet is best for you depends on the needs you have, each type of wallet is best suited to a specific purpose and personalized profile. Let's take a look at each one:

Hardware Wallet

Imagine a pendrive, a small device that connects via USB. The validation of the transfer is done by the wallet itself, its use is safe, even on infected devices.

In order to serve a better function, the private address keys, which are like the password, should be stored offline.

Paper wallets

They are simple, you only need a piece of paper where you write the private key and the public address printed or written. You don't need to leave data online that can be exposed to attacks, avoiding theft or hacking of access to assets.

However, it is important that you do not allow others to have access to the paper, because it allows you to trade your funds.

Computer Wallets

Bitcoin and other cryptocurrencies have software created to operate as wallets, some of these can be placed on the desktop allowing access to the network. There are more robust ones like Bitcoin Core, which download the entire blockchain to the computer, consuming a lot of space and internet bandwidth.

Mobile wallets

They allow you to operate anywhere and at any time. Some have options to synchronize with the computer.

When you choose a mobile wallet, you need to verify that the private key is in your possession. So that in case of a problem you can access the funds from another device or wallet.

Online Wallet

They depend on a company that is responsible for the security of the assets. In order to use them you require registration and credentials, similar to creating an email account.

Among the options you can choose Ripio, where you can see quotes, buy, sell, send and receive cryptos in a fast and secure way.

How can you choose the best wallet?

There are those who prefer to use hardware wallets to hold assets for a long time, those who want to save them and rest assured that they will not be robbed of their growing capital, for small amounts others use an online wallet.

You can always combine different wallets with different security measures according to the purpose you have with those assets. If you can, I advise you to try various forms of storage so that you can experiment with the one that suits your needs.

Difference between DeFi 1.0 and DeFi 2.0

Stage 1.0, represented by Uniswap and Sushiswap, demonstrated the powerful subversive capabilities of decentralized finance. The new financial ecology represented by decentralized exchanges is already showing its charm.

There are great results with DeFi 1.0, although also shortcomings, many projects are tokens that want to print money and this without solutions in the distribution of governance tokens and community governance. Today many technical teams are not entirely satisfied with the current decentralized and cold architecture, that's why it demanded that a decentralized, sustainable and automatically distributed financial system appears: DeFi 2.0.

Among its main advantages you can find:

•	It breaks the cold transaction mode of DeFi 1.0., seeking to establish tight horizontal connections and strong vertical links.

•	Maintain liquid mining pools active enough to participate.

•	Ecological governance and community decision-making rights. Members decide, not just based on enthusiasm and interest in participating in community activities.

•   Providing only decentralized financial services. Here are born many decentralized financial innovations that will attract global geeks to complete technological innovation ideas and explode more high-quality financial projects. Innovations in any field are going to have unlimited imagination.

Decentralized financial DeFi 2.0 is the required stage out of the 1.0 era, although the two are going to coexist in technologies, but it certainly opens up a palette of options for new investments. It's gradually going to eliminate the cold, one-off mining incentives and continue to provide a more progressive driving force and it's going to be a world of financial ecology in the future.

Are there risks involved in investing in DeFi?

Yes, it does. It is an ecosystem that has great potential, and it also has its risks:

•   There can be exorbitant movements in the price volatility of each asset.

•   Hacks could happen.

•   The ecosystem if you don't use it correctly can lead you to make mistakes that make you lose money.

•   You can lose your wallet keys if you don't use a virtual wallet like Coinbase, Binace or Bit2Me which we explain below.

•   An error in your cryptocurrency shipping address could cause you to lose your cryptocurrency.

Despite all that has been said, decentralized finance, like any interesting investment with great potential, has its risk and also its profit margin: the highest in the history of finance.

If you want to start investing you should take into account these general tips when making this type of investment:

•   Don't invest more than you can lose.

•   Diversify, don't just stick with one token or project, experiment and use different tools.

•   Store and take good care of the access keys to these decentralized tools.

- Learn, be curious, make decisions based on your own analysis of projects, technology, don't let others decide for you.

The possibilities that DeFi has are many, it is a universe in itself within the blockchain world. The potential it has is incredible and there are many changes that we will see along the way.

That's why I recommend that before you start investing, you should objectively understand the growth potential and also the risks, so you can make better decisions and even develop them.

6.   Decentralized Savings and Staking

When interest rates in the traditional world are close to zero, as they are as of the writing of this book, it's hard to generate any interest on traditional assets. If you've tried to open up a savings account to find that your interest rate is only 1 percent, or likely even less than that, how do you earn passive income? DeFi to the rescue, because there are ways that you can earn interest in one form or another on the blockchain.

There are two ways to earn interest with DeFi: one is to lend out your assets. The second way is by staking, which can potentially bring in more than with lending but of course you can also lose a lot of money by doing so. With blockchains that use Proof-of-Stake instead of Proof-of-Work, those who participate in validating the transactions earn rewards in that particular coin.

Proof-of-Work (PoW)

This is the original consensus algorithm that Bitcoin created. It's used to prove transactions and add new blocks to the chain. As you might recall from earlier, miners compete with each other to validate and get rewarded for their work.

There are two main advantages for this kind of consensus algorithm:

1. Difficult to attack: The math puzzles that must be solved to add a block to the chain are hard enough that attackers need a huge amount of computing power and a lot of time. It's not impossible, but it's certainly more difficult than, say, hacking into a computer network at the one point where everything links together.

2. "Rich" miners are not in charge: It doesn't matter how much coin you have, when mining what matters is your computations.

There are a couple of disadvantages as well:

1. It's costly in different ways: As the chains grow longer, mining new blocks requires more and more raw computational power, not to mention actual electric power. Special software is needed to solve the problems as well. Now that mining is becoming increasingly more expensive, it's also becoming more concentrated and centralized.

The software and the computations are useless for anything else. They can't be adapted for college math classes, or science data gathering. In other words, all of that power is used in only one way, which is probably not sustainable for the planet.

2. In theory, a 51 percent attack could close down the chain: When a user or user group takes over the majority of the mining operations (51 percent), they can mine all the blocks and take all the rewards by shutting out all the other miners. They can reverse transactions and create forks in the chain. Once that happens, the chain is compromised, and other users leave.

Proof-of-Stake (PoS)

An alternate algorithm, PoS was developed to address the issues of PoW. Miners can mine only the percentage of the coin they hold. For example, if a miner owns 5 percent of the available coins, then they're limited to mining 5 percent as well.

With this method, used on Ethereum and other networks, a miner would have to accumulate 51 percent of the currency, not 51 percent of the computing power. Someone who holds 51 percent of the crypto is less likely to instigate an attack against the crypto, because they would lose money as a result.

Validators for a block are randomly selected, depending on the amount they have staked.

Delegated Proof-of-Stake (DPoS)

Here's a democratic alternative to PoS invented by Daniel Larimer, a blockchain engineer who recognized that mining was too labor-intensive and too slow. He wanted a system that would be capable of 100,000 transactions per second, and PoW is too slow to accomplish that kind of speed (Crypto Stella, 2017).[1]

In DPoS, a fixed number of elected block producers (witnesses) add blocks to the chain in a round-robin type of selection order. Users vote for the witnesses, with their votes proportional to their stake, in a similar concept to PoS. Users can also choose to delegate their votes to another voter, who votes for them in the election.

Only the top witnesses are paid. There are plenty of backup witnesses since so many users are willing to take the duty. Though witnesses have a number of obligations, there's fierce competition to be one. Different platforms have varying numbers of elected witnesses; for example, Bitshare and Lisk have 101, while EOS and Steemit allow 21 witnesses.

All the competition puts some pressure on block producers to perform and make sure they're adding value. If a witness starts acting up or not adding enough value to the network, users stop voting for them, which removes them as witness. Since voting is ongoing, witnesses have constant incentive to take their duties seriously.

In addition to having elected witnesses and delegates, there are a couple of other differentiators compared to PoS. Block producers (witnesses) are the ones who create and sign new blocks. The block validators can be any user running a full node on the network. As a reminder, the block creators in PoS are referred to as validators, so the definition is different between the two.

A block is considered finalized and can't be reversed when it's finalized by 1 and ⅔ of the producers. If that doesn't happen, the next finalization is the "longest chain" rule. The longest chain is the one that most of the nodes accept as validated, and is generally the one with the most work on it. (More blocks and more work makes it more difficult for hackers to attack.)

Because the number of witnesses is limited, DPoS can handle many more transactions and is more scalable than PoW and even PoS. The price of this additional speed, however, is the centralization of the platform. Cartels could crop up, where users agree to vote for particular witnesses with the expectation that they'll be rewarded by the block producer in some way, or other means of bribing voters.

While it's an excellent solution for apps that require high throughput, centralization means it's not as secure as one that's decentralized. DPoS platforms, therefore, aren't usable as a base network like Ethereum, where platforms are built on top of its blockchain. They make sense for high-speed apps as a second layer on top of a secure platform. EOS is probably the best-known DPoS network. Others include BitShares, Steem, Ark, and Lisk.

Staking

On a blockchain that operates with PoS, you stake your coins, which allows you to participate in validating transactions (as miners do in PoW networks). Either you lock them into your wallet, or subscribe to an exchange that allows staking. You then earn a set percentage of your stake as a reward.

This is a larger market than you might expect. As staking is older than DeFi itself, in 2020 there was ten times more crypto staked than the value locked in decentralized finance (Liu, 2020).[2] Although the rewards look much better than what can be earned through lending, they vary widely between different currencies.

Staking provides a higher yield than lending crypto for the same reason that high yield (junk) bonds do compared to regular corporate bonds: it's riskier. There are three main reasons why staking carries such high returns:

Coin price volatility

Except for stablecoins, as discussed earlier, most crypto fluctuates in price with their prices able to land anywhere in a huge range. Just like in the stock market or the housing market, the idea in the cryptocurrency market is to buy low and sell high.

Your staking reward could be paid to you at a time when the coin's price is high, and you'll be disappointed when it drops.

Payment in coin

If you've ever studied the stock market, you've probably heard people tell you not to put all your eggs in one basket. If all your savings is in one stock and the company goes out of business or into bankruptcy, you've just lost all your money.

If, on the other hand, you have a portfolio of 100 stocks (maybe through owning a mutual fund) and a company goes out of business, you may have lost some money, but not all of it. In theory you might not lose any money at all, depending on the weighting of the stocks in the portfolio and how well the others performed.

The rewards for staking a coin are paid in that coin, so you're adding eggs to your one basket. If the price seems to be on a downward spiral with no hope of recovering, you're probably not going to be overjoyed with having another of the same coin.

Coin inflation

As new coins are minted, the supply is diluted, which causes inflation. Just as inflation lowers your stock or housing market returns, it reduces your currency value as well.

If you want a more consistent return for your stakes, you'll need to look for crypto with less price fluctuation and larger market cap. Do these characteristics ring a bell? They might if you've made stock investments, because in the stock market those are typically the S&P 500 stocks.

You probably think that your less risky crypto will return a lower level of rewards and you're absolutely right. In the same way that small cap stocks, which tend to be more volatile, also often earn higher returns than S&P 500 stocks, your lower-risk crypto will return less than more volatile currencies as well.

Cold staking and staking pools

You can stake a coin by yourself, using just what's in your own online wallet, on a PoS blockchain. The downside is that in order to earn the most from your stake, you have to stay connected to the network 24/7. Has your power ever gone out in the summer, winter, during a severe storm, because squirrels chewed the wires from the connection box (true story), or beavers chewed through fiber optic cables to make their dam (also a true story)? Even a brief power outage severs your connection to the network and sends you back to square one. You may be limited in your stake's earning potential if you choose to do it this way.

Another method is known as **cold staking.** Rather than storing your coin in an online wallet that must be accessible 24/7, you can store it offline in a hardware wallet. The coins must stay in that offline wallet because if you move them to a different address, you'll lose the ability to earn rewards.

Or you could join a **stakepool**. This way, you're not running the connection on your own hardware or on a virtual private network (VPN). Stakepool operators have the hardware to stay connected, generally with a master node on the blockchain that is reserved for the network only.

By joining a staking pool, not only do you not have to be concerned about local outages, but the pool's larger stake size means it's more likely to write a block or vote on it to be added to the blockchain. That gives you more of a chance to earn rewards.

Staking Requirements

How much you can make by staking varies with a number of factors, including the size of the pool, the amount of coin that's locked, and the block's rewards. The longer you **hodl** (hold on for dear life, or stake), the higher your payout will usually be, depending, of course, on the value of the coin itself. The staking rules vary according to the blockchain and the coin, so you'll want to investigate them before you decide to stake.

You might also have to run a certain operating system or other technical requirements, because you are contributing to the security of the blockchain so there usually are some minimums in terms of speed and so forth.

For the staking itself, the coin will usually specify how many you need as a minimum as well. Not every network allows cold staking in an offline wallet; your alternatives would be either staying tethered to the network 24/7/365 or joining a staking pool (if available).

You'll need an online wallet (unless you're cold staking) that supports staking. The coins you buy will normally need to season for a couple of days in your wallet before they're available for you to stake.

ETH is one of the most popular staking coins as of this writing, since staking only became possible on the chain with the December 2020 release of the first phase of the Ethereum 2.0 launch. This phase created the Beacon chain, which is the PoS chain (the first version of Ethereum is PoW). Other coins include ZCoin, Tezos, and ICON among others.

7.   Tips For Investment In Defi

As it is evident from the name, DeFi that it is a term that refers to decentralized finance. It is a network that is based on blockchain and consists of tools used by digital financial that comprise all digital securities and cryptocurrency to NFTs (Non-Fungible Tokens) and CBDCs (Central Bank Digital Currency). DeFi is a peer-to-peer financial service that licenses you to trade crypto and other relevant services. DeFi is dependent upon the Ethereum blockchain and cryptocurrencies. The DeFi market grew bigger in the year 2020. Statistics recorded raised from $700 million to $13 billion. Presently, this figure has gone up to $40 billion.

The global financial systems are evolving and transforming digitally. This displays that the DeFi financial system has a lot of potentials and can become even stronger and draw the attention of the world. But it is important that you know and understand the asset first and then how to invest in the market.

DeFi Assets

Trading DeFi assets, which are tokens representing DeFi networks, applications, or protocols, is one of the ways to invest in DeFi, this usually involves buying low and selling high. Not everyone can do this because there is a high risk involved and is extremely volatile. Nonetheless, the prospects thrive. A few examples are Uniswap (UNI), Terra (LUNA), Wrapped Bitcoin (WBTC), and Chainlink (LINK).

DeFi Staking

Another option for achieving passive income based on DeFi is staking. In staking funds are locked by users in a crypto wallet and they participate in maintaining the operations of a PoS blockchain system, which results in users getting a rate of interest that is already defined. When everyone is offering negative rates of interest, receiving a reasonable interest rate on your holdings, especially if you intend on selling them anyways is worthwhile. Assets worth a total of around $21 to $23 billion are staked on DeFi platforms, as of January 2021.

DeFi Yield Farming

Yield farming has become viral and is based on Ethereum. DeFi is an all-inclusive category of the peer-to-peer service, self-custody, KYC-less, finance apps that are based on Ethereum, but yield farming labels popular enticements program where liquidity is provided in return for a DeFi application.

DeFi Lending & Lending Protocol

Users are allowed to give away their crypto to someone else and in return earn interest on the loan on DeFi Lending platforms. Defi lending benefits lenders as well as borrowers. Not only does it offer options for margin trading, but it also enables long-term investors to lend assets and earn higher interest rates. Moreover, it also allows users to access fiat currency credit to borrow loans at lower rates than DEX. Furthermore, it can be sold by the users on a centralized exchange for a cryptocurrency and then lend to a DEX.

DeFi Funds

Trusts and Funds are another way to invest in the DeFi network. This is the most welcoming way for beginners to get acquainted with DeFi. Bitwise's DeFi Index Fund, Grayscale's Diversified DeFi fund, and Galaxy Digital's DeFi index tracker fund are some examples of DeFi funds.

Risk vs. Reward with DeFi

What makes DeFi an eye-catching and possibly profitable investment is the multiplicity of investment prospects, as well as the sustained progression of the market. However, just like with any investment, this also has risks that market investors should be made familiar with before they dive in. Not only is there a risk of the impact the crypto volatility may have but there are also security and scam risks with DeFi, that can be attributed to the DeFi protocols relying on smart contracts having weak spots that can be exploited.

The weaknesses can be decreased by the DeFi market, the technology running it, as well as the required regulations that will unavoidably be achieved, and the appeal of this digital finance system will increase. So all one has to do is be patient, be smart, and never miss a good opportunity.

Decentralized Finance (DeFi) has gathered a lot of courtesy recently. The innovation has been led by Uniswap and Compound.

Some distinguished developments include:

- DeFi market capitalization has surpassed $10 Bn
- Uniswap has outdone Coinbase

Yearn Finance has gone beyond the worth of Bitcoin for a solitary unit, it's all-time high touching the $43,000 mark.

Nonetheless, the DeFi landscape has a dark spot that is deeply hidden. The market has been tainted by rug pulls and hacks. Some people went through huge losses of money. It is significant to know the risk areas and stay safe.

Some tips to help you to take better Yield Farming decisions are given below:

1. High APY does not always guarantee high returns:

The very first thing that deceives people is high APY. For numerous projects, the opening APY is more than 10,000%. It is a great way to upsurge your money. Two questions arise:

The first one is will the High Yield be maintainable? Assess the timeline of the high yield. The supply in the early days is devaluated which results in high yields. It is halved in rapid progressions. However, this falls significantly over a short period.

The second question is will you be able to sell at a profit? Most of the time if you are able to earn a considerable amount in the early days of devaluation, you will be unable to sell the token as a majority of them will be locked. Assess the number of earned tokens you'd be able to sell.

For instance, three-quarters of Token in Luaswap is locked for initial 16 months.

2. Invest in Those Tokens That Have Authentic Use Cases:

Question yourself about why do you need the token given by the project. For many projects governance is highly overvalued. Can the token be used in any other way apart from Governance?

Are you aware of the fact that UNI can be used as collateral to get loans on other platforms? That is an actual convenience that gives UNI worth. Many other DeFi tokens are acquisitive and greedy without proper usefulness and are intended to fall.

3. Only invest in Audited Projects:

Invest in a project only and only if it is audited by a renowned organization. It is mandatory for the code of the project to be audited.

Many people invested in the yet "in production" project Eminence, when Andre Cronje revealed his connection with it due to his good reputation. But since the project was still not completed and was not audited, it was unavoidably hacked and the hacker stole $15M.

4. Inclusion of Gas Fees in your profit calculations:

It should be noted that in the present days of high gas fees the actual investment consists of the fees for buying Pair of tokens in Uniswap, accepting Liquidity Pool Pair in Uniswap, approving LP Staking in the Yield Farming Protocol, Actual Staking in Yield Farming Protocol, Unstake in Yield Farming Protocol, sell yield token in Uniswap, Removing Liquidity in Uniswap.

All these things add up to be the total fee that cannot be neglected and should always be a part of the profit calculations.

5. When Do You Plan to Enter Yield Farming project?

The time you enter a project is also very crucial because after the first few days the market inclines to fall. So it should be carefully decided when you want to enter the project. If you plan to enter a project after some time, which can be as early as a day. You cannot say that there is a selling pressure created which is from the first day's profit.

6. Take Impermanent Loss into consideration:

The amount of tokens that you have combined in the liquidity pools is adjusted by Uniswap as the worth of yield farming tokens falls. What will happen is that the amount of your yield farming token will raise and your second token (for instance ETH) will fall.

This will fall in the ratio of your unique pool submission. Your whole worth will be lower than what you would have got if you would have just held these two tokens. However, it should be noted that temporary loss is not sustained till the time the liquidity is removed. This problem can be solved by a long-time liquidity supply in the pool.

7. Don't Forget to Calculate the Price on Over-all Supply:

In the beginning, the token price is pretty high due to the low circulation but as more and more tokens are in circulation in the upcoming days. the price of the token will fall. Ascertain the position where you want your invested project to land in the CoinMarketCap ranking and try to conclude its unit price on the basis of another project with a similar supply in that CMC ranking. You will be surprised to find how low the unit price could reach!

There are high risks involved when investing in DeFi. You should only invest the amount if you are prepared for losses. Invest only in trustworthy projects. Do not invest only because of the fear of missing out. Spend some money on the cost of learning.

8.   What Is Defi Marketplace

The terms 'cryptocurrency', 'blockchain', and 'Bitcoin' have revolutionized the world entirely. Since the time when these terms were introduced tons of modernization has been witnessed in this space. DeFi is one such trend that has taken over the world of crypto over the past year, especially after BTC reached a new all-time high. Just in a short amount of time these decentralized marketplaces have made great progress, and have resulted in a very substantial modification in the world of crypto. If you are uncertain as to which DeFi marketplace is best suited for you this piece will help you figure it all out.

DeFi marketplaces are decentralized marketplaces which means that there is no middleman involved. The fundamental idea of DeFi marketplaces is very comparable to blockchain, in which the software can be downloaded by a user who can get directly linked to everyone else using the software at that instant of time.

This is how an extraordinary level of transparency is guaranteed by the platform, around the rules and working of the marketplace. Another characteristic of blockchain, which is also followed by the DeFi marketplaces is its permanence, meaning that data cannot be deleted or withdrawn by any means once it is logged into the secured system of a blockchain.

What makes DeFi marketplaces important is that centralized exchanges like Binance and Coinbase would not be used for trading if the idea of decentralization brought into view by digital currencies was better received and loved by the audiences.

Top 5 Defi Marketplaces based on Transaction Volume:

Below is a list of the top 5 decentralized marketplaces based on total trading volume concerning data from the last 30 days.

PancakeSwap

PancakeSwap is a digital exchange that was developed for the exchange of BEP20 Binance Smart Chain tokens. PancakeSwap uses the Automated market maker (AMM) model and has a market value of somewhat $16 billion.

This is how trading could be done against a liquidity pool by the users of the platform. The platform permits users to credit an amount of money into the pool, getting LP or liquidity provider tokens, which are traded for the money. The other name for the Liquidity Provider (LP) tokens is FLIP tokens.

UniSwap

UniSwap is another protocol for Ethereum's automated market maker, UniSwap also has a market value of $16 billion, just like PancakeSwap. It was launched in the year 2018, the platform is termed as a comparatively simple and smart border for swapping ERC20 tokens.

Analogous to PancakeSwap, a model has been formalized for the creation of a liquidity pool of reserves. The platform is used by liquidity providers and traders as one open-source frontend. UniSwap could be considered as a pioneer in this arena, in order to continue its leadership, it launched UniSwap v3 just recently.

MDEX

The smartest exchange innovation of recent times, MDEX is an automatic market-making decentralized exchange that functions around the fundamentals of fund pools for its users. The market volume of MDEX is well over $15 billion and it operates around Ethereum and Heco Chain.

It runs as a single hybrid platform and is a combination of the low transaction fees from the Heco chain and the vast ecosystem of Ethereum.

SushiSwap

An exchange platform based on the Ethereum blockchain network, SushiSwap is a rapidly developing DeFi marketplace. This platform has a market value of over $77 million, and it strives to encourage users to trade in crypto.

In order for it to achieve the trade goals, SushiSwap functions over the liquidity pool.

BurgerSwap

BurgerSwap is known to be the very first democratized decentralized American Metal Market (AMM), it operates on the binance smart chain. The market volume of BurgerSwap is around $51 million. BurgerSwap is one of the most noticeable and trustworthy platforms and enables any user to create proposals that let them review the transaction fees, block rewards, and make complete use of other such exchange parameters.

DeFi and blockchain function in the same way in terms of not needing any traders and the storage of transaction data on different decentralized systems. DeFi currencies serve a multitude of motives, such as easy transactions which are comparable to the functions of a virtual currency like Bitcoin. Unlike currencies like bitcoin, Defi currencies can also be used for intricate financial operations. Not only this but using DeFi marketplaces enable you to stay true to the original vision of cryptocurrencies and blockchain tech.

9.   Challenges and Risks of DeFi

Now you'll get a closer look at some of the risks that DeFi and its investors face currently.

These may change and evolve over time, depending on how the sector moves into the future. Some of the problems are likely to solve themselves if DeFi gets off the ground that it's currently on but others don't have obvious answers.

Perception is reality

For many people, decentralized finance doesn't mean anything. They may have heard of cryptocurrencies in general, and they've probably heard of Bitcoin. Both these terms, however, have a bad reputation with a lot of ordinary people who don't know much about finance or technology.

The reputational problems begin with the original whitepaper published in 2008 that posited an alternative finance solution that avoided financial institutions. The name on the whitepaper is Satoshi Nakamoto, but to this day, it's unclear whether this is an actual person or a group of people. Which is unfortunate because creating peer-to-peer alternatives is a logical reaction to many of the events leading up to the Great Recession.

At first, one of the major communities for Bitcoin was Silk Road, a marketplace on the dark web that allowed trade in anything, whether or not the item was legal. One of the biggest trading markets was for drugs, both legal and not. Silk Road was seized by the US government in 2013, and that made a big splash in the media. The message was not that Bitcoin presented an alternative to traditional finance, but that crypto enabled bad guys to do things that were illegal.

A religious friend of mine told me that she would never use cryptocurrency because it was used for human sex trafficking. That may be true or not, and certainly plenty of traffickers use fiat currency anyway; she's not alone in believing that's what crypto is used for.

The Mt. Gox scandal didn't help either. The whole premise of bitcoin, the blockchain, and distributed ledgers is security, that no one can tinker with the blocks. Magic: The Gathering Online eXchange, founded in 2010, began using Bitcoin as a currency.

In 2014, it was forced to file for bankruptcy. Users complained that they couldn't withdraw their coins, which turned out to be due to an attacker that had been draining accounts for years. This was not supposed to happen in the secure cryptocurrency world. Other thefts, such as the 2021 grab that occurred in Turkey, are also on the general public's radar.

Finally, even those who aren't attuned to the world of blockchain or crypto have seen the headlines when Bitcoin rose spectacularly in price, and also when it dropped just as spectacularly.

Investors lost a lot of their risk tolerance in and around the Great Recession, so having something called currency that is wildly unstable doesn't give them a lot of confidence. (Yes, stablecoins exist, but they're not as well-known as Bitcoin.)

In order to be taken seriously and to become a true mechanism for an alternate financial system, more people have to adopt the blockchain for themselves and their businesses. Which means that DeFi has to shed crypto's bad reputation.

That may mean doing things differently in order to capture the public's trust. The NYSE hasn't endured any theft scandals lately; neither have other stock and futures exchanges. Although crypto was also intended to avoid central banks, the Federal Reserve, Bank of England, the European Central Bank and other major central banks across the globe have not suffered anything along the lines of Mt. Gox or Silk Road either.

While crypto currently is good for speculation, average people need to trust and feel relatively safe with the system they use for their money. Right now, the blockchain is not providing them with the sense of security they need.

Relative youth

Some of the issues with DeFi are due to the relative infancy of the idea. It was only conceived this century, and we're not very far into the 21st yet. Difficulties such as high price volatility are at least partly a result of the markets still being relatively small. As more people begin to adopt the system, some of that will subside.

It's a bit of a chicken-or-egg dilemma. People don't trust crypto because it fluctuates so much, but it fluctuates so much because not enough people are in the crypto market. These types of growing pains are typical for a lot of technology, especially this century.

It also means that the theory behind the blockchain is only now being practically tested, with the expected results that the original designers didn't consider. Although, in theory, the Mt. Gox theft should have been impossible, it wasn't.

Crypto designers didn't spend enough time considering the security of all the entities that touched Bitcoin. They assumed that the block security protocols and difficulty mining blocks would solve all the problems. They were wrong.

When it comes to money, most of the public wants to know it's safe when they put it somewhere. Having a lot of people lose a lot of value because the designers didn't consider security everywhere they needed to is not exactly a recipe for trust.

New tech always has bugs. People are likely to forgive growing pains when those pains happen to a piece of software, not when bugs affect the money that they need to live on. Major financial institutions, central banks, and exchanges spend a lot of money defending against attacks and implementing new security protocols to keep a Mt. Gox from happening to them.

That's a lesson DeFi must learn if it expects to be widely adopted. What are the potential failure points, and how do you protect against them?

Cars and dot-coms in the 20th Century

DeFi is young, and youthful marketplaces and concepts often drive speculative bubbles. People get caught up in FOMO (fear of missing out) and start investing once they see prices being driven higher and higher. (Which are almost always countered by a traumatic thud when prices come back down to earth. Gravity is real.)

It also leads to a lot of innovators trying to get in on the craze, without necessarily understanding what they're doing. New technology in particular seems to convince both inventors and investors that the new marketplace is totally new and revolutionary, and that the old paradigms no longer apply. However, human nature doesn't change. More on that in the next section.

Earlier in the book you read about Warren Buffett and his comparison of the early car marketplace in the US to the dot-com boom. There were 100 car manufacturers in the early 20th Century, and towards the end there were four. If you'd invested in one car manufacturer early on, you basically had a 1-in-25 chance of picking a winner. How would you have beaten those odds? Maybe you would have gotten lucky.

When dot-coms came around, the investors who were interested were older (typically Baby Boomers) and didn't really understand the internet. The inventors thought they knew everything, especially once the investors started throwing money at any web address that ended in dotcom. However, the laws of supply and demand don't change just because a new technology has entered the Thunderdome. And so the bubble ended in a predictable crash.

Even in the early 2000s, people set aside long-known investment truths to throw themselves into a frenzy. There is a lot of blame to go around for the Great Recession, everything from government policies to individual greed to corporate greed.

Once the floodgates opened, everyone could buy their own house that they couldn't afford in reality, thanks to forged documents and NINJA loans (no job, no income or assets) from questionable lenders and their suppliers.

The idea was that homeowners could buy a bigger house with a lower interest rate loan, paying the interest only, and then refinancing when the principal payments started. This presupposed that housing prices, which had recently begun to blow the roof, would keep going up. Which is not at all how finance works - no market continues to rise indefinitely - but people chose to ignore this inconvenient fact.

The banks got busy creating mortgage loan packages for their greedy investors - interest rates had fallen and investors were searching for yield. The banks didn't even know what they were doing, and very few, if any, of the officers responsible for creating these mortgage packages (known as CMOs and CDOs) understood the math.

The mortgage originators didn't care that their loans were unlikely to perform. They knew the banks would buy the worst mortgage and stuff it into a package and sell it to investors. That's decentralization (in a way) for you, and it ended very, very badly for the potential homeowners and all the people who lost jobs in the ensuing recession.

Currently, at least in crypto (as opposed to blockchain or DeFi), there are a bunch of people who don't know what they're doing and investors (and inventors) who have joined in the latest frenzy. After all, we are in a low interest rate environment, and holding coins can bring you more yield than what you'll find at a bank or in a bond. As the saying goes (usually attributed to Mark Twain), "History never repeats itself but it often rhymes."[1]

You'll note that cars continue to be driven, some dotcoms have become enormous enterprises that employ thousands of people, and people continue to take out mortgages. The question is whether DeFi is pre- or post-bubble. If it's pre-bubble, then it makes sense for investors and average people to wait until the market shakes out and separates the companies with a good chance of succeeding from those that don't.

Human nature and centralization

It may come as a surprise to many libertarians, but many of the rules and regulations around traditional finance were designed to prevent abuses and issues experienced in the past. They're not (usually) made up just to frustrate people.

Some people rail about the Federal Reserve and its power. It was chartered in the early 20th Century and originally designed to maintain full employment (which is not the same as 100 percent employment, by the way.) It only received inflation-fighting power after the oil crisis led to stagflation in the 1970s.

Licensing requirements for stockbrokers and insurance sellers are there to ensure that the people selling financial products have at least a tiny bit of familiarity with how the markets work and what's legal and what's not. That's because in the 1920s there were too many snake-oil salesmen selling phony stock certificates and other fraud schemes to credulous investors.

Selling snake oil with no compunction, making a buck off a credulous mark, and ignoring the consequences of your actions are fundamental to capitalism, especially in the United States. When the consequences are dangerous and/or life-threatening, however, the government arguably has a responsibility to address them.

For example, California's tighter emissions standards aren't because Californians hate cars. Los Angeles is completely surrounded and bisected by huge freeways, because it became a major city after cars became popular. LA's geography means smog from vehicle exhaust gets trapped over the city and its environs, especially on hot days. The state tightened emissions standards so Californians could breathe. Los Angeles County is one of the largest in the country in terms of population, so without the standards a lot of people would have needlessly died.

Note, however, that the tighter standards are due to government intervention. Conventional libertarian wisdom holds that the free market solves all problems, but that's prima facie wrong. The car manufacturers didn't voluntarily decide to make engines cleaner so people could breathe.

The tobacco industry knew that their product was poisonous and led to early death for decades, but they tried to squash the release of that information. The invisible hand of the market allowed them to continue to sicken and kill people, until the documents came to light. Even so, the government had to intervene by restricting tobacco advertising to children and taking other measures.

In other words, the 20th and 21st Centuries have shown that there are bad actors out there and that the free market doesn't always solve the problem, even though it should in theory. People want to have a place where they can go to complain or get their problems straightened out. Automated bots don't do it; people want to actually talk to someone to get their problem solved, especially when it comes to money.

Centralized exchanges and platforms have this capability. On the other hand, that goes against the ethos of decentralization in the first place! While centralization would no doubt appeal to many ordinary people who are concerned about not having anyone to turn to when something goes wrong, other users will want to ensure that the blockchain remains decentralized. If it doesn't catch on with the public, many of the current problems (such as lack of liquidity) will remain.

Competitive landscape: traditional system

You've seen how much a decentralized system with fewer intermediaries can potentially benefit people across the globe by giving them more access to capital without needing a sizable chunk of money to begin with.

The existing traditional players have a lot of power and they're closely linked with government structures as well. Any alternative that's going to be widely adopted has to be recognized as being just as secure as the existing structure, and DeFi currently is not.

You might think (or hope) that the failure of governments and banking institutions during the Great Recession might have an effect on people who use the current system. After all, only one (foreign) banker in the US went to jail, and none of the others did. In fact, some of the banks that played a big part in the meltdown are stronger than ever.

Depending on your political beliefs, there are easy scapegoats on the "other" side: conservatives blame greedy homeowners and the government for loosening lending standards. Liberals blame the mortgage companies who made bad loans and the banks who packaged the loans. The underlying structure, however, has largely escaped comment, at least among the general public and the media. Most people are not blaming the centralized system for being the culprit.

Not to mention that the existing system already has a lot of political power, in addition to money. Its members regularly lobby the government, and because of their deep pockets, they're the ones to listen to.

Can you buy, for example, Facebook's Libra coin? Recall that it was pulled due to concerns that it would affect the traditional system. If you're considering a cryptocurrency that's usable around the world it's not a bad idea to base it on a basket of currencies, not just the US dollar or euro or yuan.

That's not a terrible business model. Although you can certainly argue that an entity other than a social media company known for privacy invasion should launch it. It was pulled, not because it wouldn't succeed, but because it might succeed too well.

The blockchain will need to figure out a way to work around the power structure coziness to attract more business.

Competitive landscape: apps

There already is an arena that cuts down on intermediaries and costs, and uses automation to simplify financial transactions. It's known as **fintech**, which is the universe of financial apps that are available to many users around the globe.

There are apps to help people looking for insurance policies to compare and contrast policies from a variety of companies. You can get a term life insurance quote in seconds. You can deposit checks by taking pictures of them on your phone instead of hitting the teller or even the ATM. You can pay bills automatically from your checking account, or even your rewards credit card.

If you're a business owner, there are already automated payroll systems and HR departments. You can hire a CFO, COO, accountant, etc., on a consulting basis and pull up their bios immediately to see if you want to hire them.

From a user perspective, these companies are already regulated in most countries. There's no need to change to a widely fluctuating currency to take advantage of automation and machine learning to get a loan, for example. That means if something goes wrong you have a number to call, which the average person really wants in a service provider.

Human error (developers)

Tech works really well - when it's working! We've all been at a store when their connection goes down or their automated sales system stops working or had some issue with software, etc. Almost every software release goes out with bugs, because the prevailing culture is to just ship it and let the users tell you about the bugs. Again, people are often willing to deal with it when it comes to software but not necessarily when that software is dealing with their money.

There's no guarantee that a developer creating smart contracts can make sure they're bug-free. Things often get missed, even when you're working with open-source code or programs designed to be easily read, like Go programming language. Of course, there's no manager to call if the auto-execute feature doesn't work like it was supposed to.

For example, suppose that an investor buys an option contract on blockchain which is designed to automatically run if the option's in the money at expiration. A bug prevents the program from executing. The user on the other side of the trade might not mind, but that investor will. Who do they go to?

It's not the other side's fault that the 3rd party smart contract didn't work, so they're not going to make the investor whole. Who will? The developer? Will the investor even know who the developer is? Some platforms offer insurance, but what if the users decide they don't want to pay out that claim? That's the kind of uncertainty that investors are not willing to risk money on.

Human error (users)

In theory, pushing authority down the chain is the most democratic thing to do, and it (theoretically) makes sense for the end user to have more control over their financial tech. That's not always how it works best in practice, though!

Consider California's ballot initiatives. They were conceived as a way for the voter to register their personal preferences on issues that achieve a certain amount of signatures, rather than having the elected representatives make those decisions. Great idea, in theory.

Most people in the 21st Century are awash in information overload. The 2020 election included 26 ballot initiatives, many of them confusingly named. In some cases, if you supported Cause X, you would actually have to vote against the ballot measure named Save Cause X.

Even if you read the voter information guide, it's a lot to wade through. Many people don't have or want to take the time to wade through it, and so they rely on sound bites or what their friends told them about it.

In a similar vein, there are still people (and not all of them over 65) who look frantically for the "any" key when they're on a tech support call. Giving them more authority over their tech choices might not actually help them make better decisions, as much as we'd like to think it would.

Poor user experiences

Most blockchain users currently are at least reasonably tech-savvy, and can figure out what they need to know or do when presented with an interface that isn't intuitive. Though they may still be annoyed when things are taking too long to wind their way onto a block, or the system is otherwise slow in processing something.

In order for more people to adopt the technology, it has to be friendlier to people who aren't tech savvy. You've probably heard the howls of outrage every time a social media platform changes the format of something its users like. Even if the GUI is simpler, it still takes time for the public to get used to it and get comfortable with it.

People won't use something that's too hard to navigate. If they have to wrap their heads not only around the idea of blockchain itself, and then figure out how to use a particular platform, they're going to give up and go back to the app or their bank where they know how to get things done. Blockchain developers need to take the next step of not just focusing on how to solve a particular problem, but to make it easy for people to get the answer.

Poor performance

Blockchain processing can take longer than similar processes in the traditional system, due to the large number of nodes that are involved. Centralized systems don't rely on tens or hundreds of computers scattered around the globe, and their transaction times are therefore usually much faster.

While some networks boast of their performance speeds of so many transactions (tx) per second, that's usually in a controlled environment with a much more limited number of nodes than what real-world users experience.

Higher transaction costs

Clients (or users) of DeFi do a lot of the computational work through decentralized systems. While the blockchain platforms are faster and lighter, it may take a user's computer some time to actually perform the calculations and get the digital signatures necessary for game or wallet transactions.

The more layers of cryptography (that secure the transactions), the longer it takes. From the user's perspective, it slows them down.

P2P networking

In essence, information on one transaction is sent twice: once from the user to the block producer, which may distribute it out to a group of peers. Then back to the user once confirmed, which may use a completely different set of peers to validate.

Because the paths are randomly distributed, they can't be optimized for performance the way transactions in the traditional system can. Their networks are designed and built for speed. While a decentralized system is safer from malicious participants and central points of failure, it can't guarantee any kind of data transfer performance.

This part of the process can also be very time-consuming on the blockchain, which many users will understand as bad performance from the system.

Consensus algorithm

Whether PoS or PoW algorithms are used, mining and voting take time. If the platform or network is having some kind of tech issue, there will be more delays.

The more participants on a blockchain, the slower it will be. The ability to scale up is something developers are currently working on. Ethereum's use of shards may help to solve this part of the problem and speed up the transfers, resulting in a better experience for the users.

Liquidity issues

As noted earlier, this is somewhat of a chicken-or-egg conundrum. Crypto markets tend to be illiquid because there aren't as many participants but of course people don't want to participate in a market with no liquidity!

Why is liquidity so important? It may not be an issue for early adopters, investors who already have plenty of liquid assets elsewhere, or speculators who don't mind taking on enormous amounts of risk. Many people (especially in the US) live paycheck to paycheck, and one of their biggest problems is the lack of cash in case of emergencies (Roberts, 2020).[2]

The general public wants to be able to access their money when they need it. If they lose their jobs, or the house needs an unexpected repair, or whatever the issue might be, they don't want their funds sitting in a market where they can't get to them. Or a market where one day their holdings are worth $5,000 and the next $500.

Paper (or digital) wealth is great to look at. If you can't transform your millions in crypto into a reasonable equivalent in fiat currency, crypto isn't actually worth very much. While stablecoins may be more liquid, you can't earn very much with them, at least compared to other kinds of coins.

Investors ask for higher rates of return for illiquid investments; after all, they're riskier. The cryptocurrency world needs some mechanism to reliably deliver the higher rates if the markets stay small, in order to compensate the investors for taking on an illiquid investment.

Sustainability

The fact is that the earth is getting warmer due to human activity. The Greenhouse Effect is due to the Earth's atmosphere trapping heat that would otherwise dissipate out into space. Certain gases that have increased due to human activity contribute to the effect, including methane, nitrous oxide (NO), and carbon dioxide (CO2). Burning fossil fuels results in much more NO and CO2, which makes the planet heat up faster. While three degrees warmer doesn't seem like it could do much damage, it would cause glaciers to melt and a number of coastal cities would disappear underwater, such as Osaka, Shanghai, Rio de Janeiro, and Miami (Holder et al, 2017).[3] Land that is now used to grow food will no longer support agriculture because the temperatures will be too hot. And so on.

Blockchains that use mining and PoW algorithms use a lot of power, much of which is generated by burning fossil fuels like oil and coal. That's not a sustainable practice, not to mention that many people who are concerned about the environment will refuse to use it. (Remember the artists who pulled back NFTs due to climate concerns.)

Fortunately, one solution is PoS consensus that doesn't require massive amounts of power to build and validate blocks. The general public will need to be educated about the difference, because if all they know is Bitcoin and mining, they'll be worried about blockchain's effect on the Earth.

Blockchain can actually be a force for good when it comes to the environment. Using it for the supply chain means less waste, and traceability means less fraud and fewer natural resources devoted to fraudulent transactions and products.

The networks, however, have to be PoS and not PoW. What happens to Bitcoin? It's not sustainable. The network has constrained the system to mine only 21 billion coins in total, and as of this writing slightly less than 19 million have been mined.

Due to the way Bitcoins are structured, it's not expected that the last one will be mined until 2140 (Phillips et al, 2021). By then, unless things change significantly, the earth will be experiencing serious issues with warming as discussed above.

As long as DeFi remains on PoS networks, they won't be contributing to global warming. If Bitcoin doesn't change the way it runs, that might not matter. When catastrophe arrives, it doesn't really matter how we got there.

Practical Tools in Decentralized Finance Risk

- Use data in Ethereum blockchain with Etherscan.

Etherscan, an Ethereum Blockchain network Explorer website, is a handy tool for examining transactions and the condition of the Ethereum Blockchain network. It may be used to look up and verify any trade or transaction on the blockchain network. The majority of blockchain networks have their explorer.

It is advised that you use Etherscan to monitor the wallet transactions and input your Ethereum wallet address. Examine the recipient addresses of any recent transactions you've done, and if there are any odd situations, like any bizarre behavior, address them as soon as feasible.

- Use Coingecko to get the most recent information on cryptocurrencies as well as the most recent price changes

This is a very handy tool for getting full and reference information on different currencies, as well as price fluctuations and market capacity. You may also utilize Coingecko to get the most up-to-date information on liquidity and Farming Pools, as well as the current APY, the number of audits linked with that platform, and the total value locked.

You can get the most detailed information about liquidity pools in various blockchain networks by utilizing the LiquidityFolio platform. You may also verify your presence in multiple pools by inputting the wallet address into this platform.

- The Zapper platform aims to make fund management easier in decentralized finance.

A Defi fund management program aims to deliver services on decentralized finance platforms so that all assets may be viewed in the dashboard. Furthermore, the platform aims to simplify it by offering the most significant liquidity, Farm pools, and relevant filters.

- Use the Zerion platform to conduct all key activities in Defi via a good user interface.

It is a useful tool for controlling all critical processes in the Defi ecosystem. Using this platform, you may track your portfolio in a chart format that is very useful and thorough in presenting portfolio assets. It even keeps track of NFT assets. The fact that this platform has a nice user interface is one of its most significant features.

There are additional parts for Exchange, Borrow, and a search bar for key liquidity pools and YF sites on the network. Another benefit of these platforms is their partnerships with DEXs and the simplicity they may conduct transactions.

For instance, during the initial 1inch Airdrop, the 1Inch platform that distributed 600 tokens to its participants had some initial delays owing to increased traffic from participants claiming coins and requesting transfers to their wallets. Participants that checked the 1Inch Twitter account and learned about the system's connection with Zerion, on the other hand, were able to move Airdrop coins to their Zerion wallet quickly.

- The YF Tools platform offers significant Defi-related tools and resources.

This tool includes features like estimating the Impermanent Loss, the size of Collateral, and more. One of the benefits of this platform is that it allows you to learn about the most significant and current issues in decentralized finance, which can be found in the Resource section.

You may use the Impermanent Loss estimator equally and obtain the most recent Ethereum gas Fees under the Tools section. This platform includes a liquidity pool search bar. However, it differs in that it has extremely great and unique filters. Filters like APY rates, smart contract risk, and Impermanent Loss, as well as numerous platforms which provide decentralized finance, collateral type, and coins in Pools, and benefits for participation in different Pools, are all extremely helpful.

- Trade through the @GaspriceTrackerBot bot on Telegram, and set notification for the right time.

This bot is designed to give recent information about Ethereum Blockchain network transaction costs. This bot can also send out notifications when fees are low or warnings when the gas fee charges are high.

- Use the Gasnow site to get the optimal gas fee for you based on the time priority that is most convenient for you before conducting any transactions on the Ethereum blockchain network.

This site, which is backed by Sparkpool, one of the largest Ethereum network mining pools, provides the most exact amount of gas fees in four distinct periods. Another benefit of this site is that it provides a helpful chart of the amount of gas fee vs the number of completed transactions that can forecast the traffic on the Ethereum blockchain.

- Determine the risk profile of smart contracts and helper tools by visiting Defiyield-.info

It is with no question among the most crucial decentralized finance management systems. This tool may look for liquidity pools and Vaults from other platforms to invest in. One of the essential aspects of Defiyield is that it displays the audits that have been completed and the risk level of smart contracts in the decentralized finance landscape.

It equally contains the Impermanent Loss estimator, which has the most precise and user interface. Stopping Ethereum Network Transactions and a Gas Cost Monitor are two other significant features of this platform.

- Use lending management features with the Defisaver platform.

It's among the most crucial instruments in the loan and borrowing landscape. We could effectively safeguard our Collateral against loans acquired from various sites due to this technology, giving us peace of mind.

We may also return our loan by generally making just a single transaction, which saves us money on trading costs. Another helpful function of this platform is the ability to transform collaterals to one another or move your holdings from one network to another in a single transaction. In addition, when a participant launches Smart wallet on the platform, a Maker CDP is immediately generated for them.

You may equally apply the Loan Shifter function after developing a smart wallet. In brief, DefiSaver lowers trading costs in the lending and borrowing landscape while also making fund and collateral management super simple.

- Benefit from the new decentralized finance services in lending by using the Instadapp platform.

The platform has also shown to be highly beneficial in the lending industry and strategy execution. Instadapp is recognized for its unique approach to participant service in this domain.

The use of Uniswap LP coins in leverage and collateral strategies, for instance, is highly intriguing and creative in the most recent upgrade of its services. Professional decentralized finance participants have been able to boost their revenue via the fees of AMM platforms thanks to this innovative approach.

- Furucombo allows you to do several transactions in one.

The platform is intended for participants already acquainted with Defi and want to make complicated hybrid transactions easier. Furucombo allows you to perform a set of complicated decentralized finance protocols strategies in one transaction. You may equally gain ideas from other example combinations in the Explore area and utilize them to optimize your trades.

- You may browse and get rapid and classified access to decentralized applications by utilizing dappradar.

With the proliferation of decentralized apps on various blockchain networks, classified access and exploration using realistic filters are becoming increasingly important.

This platform serves as a conduit between blockchain network developers and participants. Statistical reporting, fund management, and recent information on NFT markets are among the other advantages of this platform.

10. Problems Defi Solves

This chapter addresses DeFi's concrete solutions to the five flaws of traditional finance: inefficiency, limited access, opacity, centralized control, and lack of interoperability.

INEFFICIENCY

The first of the five flaws of traditional finance is inefficiency. DeFi can handle financial transactions with high volumes of assets and low friction that would generally be a large organizational burden for traditional finance. It does this by creating dApps: reusable smart contracts designed to execute a specific financial operation and available to any user who seeks that type of service, for example, to execute a put option, regardless of the size of the transaction. A user can largely self-serve within the parameters of the smart contract and of the blockchain the application lives on. In the case of Ethereum-based DeFi, the contracts can be used by anyone who pays the flat gas fee, currently around \$3 for a transfer and \$12 for a dApp feature such as leveraging against collateral. Once deployed, these contracts continually provide their service with near-zero organizational overhead.

Keepers

Keepers are external participants directly incentivized to provide a service to DeFi protocols, such as monitoring positions to safeguard that they are sufficiently collateralized or triggering state updates for various functions. To ensure that a dApp's benefits and services are optimally priced, keeper rewards are often structured as an auction. Pure, open competition provides value to DeFi platforms by guaranteeing users pay the market price for the services they need.

Forking

Another concept that also incentivizes efficiency is a **fork**. In the context of open-source code, this occurs when the code is copied and reused with upgrades or enhancements layered on top. A common fork in blockchain protocols is formed when they are referenced in two parallel currencies and chains. Doing so creates competition at the protocol level and creates the best possible smart contract platform. Not only is the code of the entire Ethereum blockchain public and forkable, but each DeFi dApp built on top of Ethereum is as well. Should inefficient or suboptimal DeFi applications exist, the code can be easily copied, improved, and redeployed through forking. Forking and its benefits arise from the open nature of DeFi and blockchains.

Forking creates an interesting challenge to DeFi platforms, namely, **vampirism**: an exact or near-carbon copy of a DeFi platform designed to poach liquidity or users by offering larger incentives than the platform it is copying. Users might be attracted to the higher potential reward for the same functionality, which would cause a reduction in usage and liquidity on the initial platform.

If the inflationary rewards are flawed, with prolonged use the clone could perhaps collapse after a large asset bubble or could select closer-to-optimal models and replace the original platform. Vampirism is not an inherent risk or flaw but rather a complicating factor arising from the pure competition and openness of DeFi. The selection process will eventually give rise to more robust financial infrastructure with optimal efficiency.

LIMITED ACCESS

As smart contract platforms move to more scalable implementations, user friction falls, enabling a wide range of users and thus mitigating the second flaw of traditional finance: limited access. DeFi gives large, underserved groups like the global unbanked population and small businesses that employ substantial portions of the workforce (e.g., nearly 50 percent in the United States) direct access to financial services. The resulting impact on the entire global economy should be strongly positive. Even consumers who have access to traditional financial services such as bank accounts, mortgages, and credit cards cannot get products with the most competitive pricing and most favorable terms because they are restricted to large institutions. DeFi allows all users access to the entirety of its financial infrastructure, regardless of their wealth or geographic location.

Yield Farming

Yield farming provides access to many who need financial services but whom traditional finance leaves behind. It provides users with inflationary or contract-funded rewards for staking capital or using a protocol, which are then payable in the same underlying asset the user holds or in a distinct asset such as a governance token. Any user can participate, staking an amount of any size – regardless of how small – and receiving a proportional reward. This capability is particularly powerful in the case of governance tokens. A user of a protocol that issues a governance token via yield farming becomes a partial owner of the platform through the issued token. A rare occurrence in traditional finance, this process is a common and celebrated way to give ownership of the platform to the people who use and benefit from it.

Initial DeFi Offering

An interesting consequence of yield farming is that a user can create an **initial DeFi offering** (IDO) by market making their own Uniswap trading pair. They can set the initial exchange rate by becoming the first liquidity provider on the pair. Suppose the user's token is called DFT and has a total supply of 2 million. They can make each DFT worth 0.10 USDC by opening the market with 1 million DFT and 100,000 USDC. Any ERC20 token holder can purchase DFT, which drives up the price. As the only liquidity provider, the user also receives all the trading fees. In this way, they can get their token immediate access to as many users as possible. The method sets an artificial price floor for the token if the user controls the supply outside of the amount supplied to the Uniswap market and, as such, inhibits price discovery. The trade-offs of an IDO should be weighed as an option, or strategy, for a user's token distribution.

IDOs democratize access to DeFi in two ways. First, an IDO allows a project to list on high-traffic DeFi exchanges that do not have barriers to entry beyond the initial capital. Second, an IDO allows a user access to the best new projects immediately after the project lists.

OPACITY

The third drawback of traditional finance is opacity. DeFi elegantly solves this problem through the open and contractual nature of agreements. We will explore how smart contracts and tokenization improve transparency within DeFi.

Smart Contracts

Smart contracts provide an immediate benefit in terms of transparency. All parties are aware of the capitalization of their counterparties and, to the extent required, can see how funds will be deployed. They can each read the contract, agree on the terms, and eliminate any ambiguity. This transparency substantially eases the threat of legal burdens and brings peace of mind to smaller players who, in the current environment of traditional finance, could be abused by powerful counterparties through delaying or even completely withholding their end of a financial agreement. Realistically, the average consumer does not understand the contract code but can rely on the open-source nature of the platform, the existence of code audits (discussed later) and the wisdom of the crowd to feel secure. Overall, DeFi mitigates counterparty risk and thus creates a host of efficiencies not present under traditional finance.

DeFi participants are accountable for acting in accordance with the terms of the contracts they use. One mechanism for ensuring the appropriate behavior is **staking**, in which a cryptoasset is escrowed into a contract and released to the appropriate counterparty only after the terms are met or is returned to the original holder. Parties can be required to stake on any claims or interactions they make. Staking enforces agreements by imposing a tangible penalty for the misbehaving side and a tangible reward for the counterparty, the latter of which should be as good as or even better than the outcome of the original terms of the contract. These transparent incentive structures provide much more secure and more obvious guarantees than traditional financial agreements.

Another type of smart contract in DeFi that improves transparency is a **token contract**, which allows users to know exactly how many tokens are in the system and the parameters of inflation and deflation.

CENTRALIZED CONTROL

The fourth flaw of traditional finance is the strong control exerted by governments and large institutions that hold a virtual monopoly over elements such as the money supply, rate of inflation, and access to the best investment opportunities. DeFi upends this centralized control by relinquishing control to open protocols with transparent and immutable properties. The community of stakeholders or even a predetermined algorithm can control a DeFi dApp's parameter, such as the inflation rate. If a dApp contains special privileges for an administrator, all users are aware of the privileges, and any user can readily create a less centralized competitor.

The open-source ethos of blockchain and the public nature of all smart contracts assures that flaws and inefficiencies in a DeFi project can be readily identified and "forked away" by users who copy and improve the flawed project. Consequently, DeFi strives to design protocols that naturally and elegantly incentivize stakeholders and maintain a healthy equilibrium through careful mechanism design. Naturally, there are trade-offs in having and not having a centralized party. Centralized control allows for radically decisive action in a crisis, which may or may not be the appropriate reaction. The path to decentralizing finance will certainly involve growing pains because of the challenges in pre-planning for every eventuality and economic nuance. Ultimately, however, the transparency and security a decentralized approach brings will lead to robust protocols that can become trusted financial infrastructure for a global user base.

Decentralized Autonomous Organization

In a **decentralized autonomous organization** (DAO), the rules of operation are encoded in smart contracts that determine who can execute what behavior or upgrade. It is common for a DAO to have some kind of **governance token**, which gives an owner some percentage of the vote on future outcomes. We will explore governance in much more detail later.

LACK OF INTEROPERABILITY

We will now touch on how DeFi solves for the lack of interoperability that exists in traditional finance. Traditional financial products are difficult to integrate, generally requiring at minimum a wire transfer and many cases unable to be recombined. The possibilities for DeFi are substantial, and new innovations continue to grow exponentially, fueled by how easy it is to compose DeFi products. Once a base infrastructure has been established – for example, to create a synthetic asset – any new protocols allowing for borrowing and lending can be applied. A higher layer would allow for attainment of leverage on top of borrowed assets. Such composability can continue in an increasing number of directions as new platforms arise. For this reason, **DeFi Legos** is an analogy often used to describe the act of combining existing protocols into a new protocol. The next section discusses tokenization and networked liquidity, which are advantages to this composability.

Tokenization

Tokenization is a critical way DeFi platforms integrate. Take, for example, a percentage ownership stake in a private commercial real estate venture. It would be quite difficult in traditional finance to use this asset as collateral for a loan or as margin to open a levered derivative position. Because DeFi relies on shared interfaces, applications can directly plug into each other's assets, repackage, and subdivide positions as needed. DeFi has the potential to unlock liquidity in traditionally illiquid assets through tokenization. A simple use case would be creating fractional shares from a unitary asset such as a stock. We can extend this concept to give fractional ownership to scarce resources such as rare art. The tokens can be used as collateral for any other DeFi service, such as leverage or derivatives.

We can invert this paradigm to create token bundles of groups of real-world or digital assets and trade them like an ETF. Imagine a dApp like a real estate investment trust (REIT), but with the added capability of allowing the owner to subdivide the REIT into the individual real estate components to select a preferred geographic distribution and allocation within the REIT. Owning the token means overseeing how the properties are distributed. The token can be traded on a decentralized exchange to liquidate the position.

Compared with digital assets, tokenizing hard assets, such as real estate or precious metals, is more difficult because the practical considerations such as maintenance and storage cannot be enforced by code. Legal restrictions across jurisdictions are also a challenge for tokenization; nevertheless, the utility of secure, contractual tokenization for most use cases should not be underestimated.

A tokenized version of a position in a DeFi platform is a pluggable derivative asset that is usable in another platform. Tokenization allows the benefits and features of one position to be portable. The archetypal example of portability through tokenization is Compound, which allows for robust lending markets in which a position – itself a token – can accrue variable-rate interest denominated in a given token. If, for example, the base asset is ETH, the ETH deposit wrapper known as cETH (cToken) can be used in place of the base asset. The result is an ETH-backed derivative that is also accruing variable-rate interest per the Compound protocol. Tokenization therefore unlocks new revenue models for dApps because they can plug asset holdings directly into Compound or use the cToken interface to gain the benefits of Compound's interest rates.

Networked Liquidity

The concept of interoperability extends easily to liquidity in the exchange use case. Traditional exchanges – in particular those that retail investors typically use – cannot readily share liquidity with other exchanges. In DeFi, as a subcomponent of the contract, any exchange application can leverage the liquidity and rates of any other exchange on the same blockchain. This capability allows for networked liquidity and leads to very competitive rates for users within the same application.

11. The Future Of Decentralized Finance (Defi)

Before we proceed, let's take a brief look at some of the things Defi enables us to do:

- Transparency: A financial environment that is transparent and auditable.

- Accessibility: Unrestricted access to Defi apps without fear of discrimination based on race, gender, beliefs, nationality, or geographic location.

- Efficient: Programmable money allows for the elimination of centralized middlemen, resulting in a more economical and efficient financial market.

- Convenience: For a modest price and with little waiting time, money may now be transmitted anywhere, at any time, and to anybody who has access to a cryptocurrency wallet.

All of those mentioned above have enabled users to accomplish the following: supply liquidity to earn yields on unproductive assets with no maturation/lock-in period, obtain loans (with collateral) without paperwork and repay them whenever they want, and quickly execute automated trading methods. The best part is that all of the above may be accessible by anybody, anywhere, anytime, as long as they have Internet connectivity. That is the power of Defi in terms of accessibility, and we are only at the beginning of this adventure.

According to the blockchain platform Dune Analytics statistics, the number of Defi users climbed from 93,000 in January 2020 to 1.8 million in April 2021. The market's valuation climbed from $700 million to $58 billion during the same period. Despite emerging to the surface during a stock market meltdown and a pandemic, decentralized finance became the industry's next big thing. Defi transcended its niche status and completely dispelled the worry of becoming another ICO-like phenomenon. Furthermore, its vicious performance was frightening enough to frighten crypto's centralized exchanges, which have lost a major portion of liquidity to DEXs.

DeFi's disruptive potential is undeniable. A new decentralized future is upon us, which should come as no surprise in the blockchain sector. However, there are other challenges that must be addressed before we can achieve widespread adoption.

Smart contracts continue to be vulnerable to exploits, anonymous developers continue to act like vultures by starting rug pull initiatives, and the threat of laws continues to loom over our heads. For the time being, Defi is the wild west of crypto, and both creators and users must reach a specific degree of maturity for the specialized ecosystem to establish itself as a prominent and serious sector in this new decade.

It will take several years to achieve a perfected and balanced state, and the timing will be fully dependent on the community and its conduct. In these unpredictable and chaotic times, it seems apparent that disruptive technologies are more likely than ever to enter the actual world and that this is our opportunity to make significant changes. The road may be long and difficult, but one thing is certain: the future of finance is decentralized.

Individual users will not wish to conduct their transactions across several platforms. Users will mostly congregate around on-ramps (for example, exchanges) and wallets (e.g., balance.io). Because these initiatives are open-source and decentralized, they will be able to interface with one another to enable trade, storage of existing assets, insurance, and other functions within the same platform. We're seeing some early variants of this, such as Trust Wallet interacting with Dapps. Platforms such as Morpher.io and Abra are beginning to integrate traditional instruments such as equities with tokens, which will play a significant role in allowing people in remote parts of the world to gain access to previously unattainable foreign assets. De-Fi platforms may, over time, reduce the complexity created by regulators in the goal of keeping economies walled off, allowing regular investors without the appropriate instruments (e.g., specialist banks) to gain access to commodities, exotic assets, derivatives, foreign currencies, and even equity.

The Defi ecosystem as a whole is estimated to be worth roughly $1 billion. Today, the majority of this is provided through MakerDAO. If we use token market capitalization as a proxy, it is worth less than 1% of the overall ecosystem, based on the total market capitalization of $173 billion. However, decentralized banking is one of the few areas where a tokenized product is used regularly. It can restore utility tokens' "utility." Decentralized finance has the potential to enable applications that were thought to be achievable in 2013 but difficult to develop due to scaling issues and volatility. The advent of reliable tokens, payment systems, and lending platforms might create opportunities for businesses worldwide and bring our financial markets closer together while enhancing transparency. While there is significant systemic danger in these systems (e.g., Dai locked up with eth, used to buy Eth), they provide an alternative to the banks, which may have put an entire generation in jeopardy with their CDOs in 2008. It is far too early to declare any of them the clear victors. However, it may be premature to conclude that Defi will not add value to the ecosystem.

When entrepreneurs traveled far and wide in pursuit of new opportunities 400 years ago, they issued stock as a method for individuals to share the risks and rewards of new companies. It democratized access to wealth-creation tools. When Satoshi Nakamoto released the Bitcoin code ten years ago, he developed a financial system that ensured an individual's money stayed theirs.

Decentralized finance is the natural progression of the same. It has the potential to bring our markets closer together than ever before, to eliminate needless middlemen, to provide significant cost efficiencies, and to open access to populations that have previously been underserved.

It, like the web, will first serve a privileged few, but its benefits will be passed on to an entire generation of underserved consumers who may never have had access to loans or the ability to make international payments. If macro trends such as the gig economy and globalization continue, the necessary financial infrastructure must be put in place.

We have our first true shot at making it happen with decentralized money. When Satoshi published Bitcoin's whitepaper, banks were on the verge of yet another bailout. Decentralized finance expands on his idea of providing individuals with dignity, sovereignty, and transparency over the storage and investment of their hard-earned money. It isn't the establishment's anti-banking stance. It is the consumer-friendly option.

And by constructing it, one is not undermining the power of the government or banks but rather enabling the common man to have an option in an ecosystem where none has existed for millennia.

The Defi User Experience

While access to Defi apps may be a non-issue, the whole user experience remains one of DeFi's key pain points. Having said that, numerous teams throughout the world are working hard to improve the experience. Examine some of them and the problems they are seeking to solve:

Wallet: Argent is developing a dramatically improved user-focused crypto wallet experience, including free Ethereum transactions without the requirement for ETH, native integration with Compound (and others), and the elimination of seed keys.

Product participation: DeFiZap abstracts away many of the intricacies and stages required with Defi products, allowing customers to access various financial products in a single transaction, saving time and effort.

Gelato Finance has announced their "If this, then that" cryptocurrency development. It essentially allows users to define actions that will be carried out when specific criteria are satisfied, such as "Buy ETH when it is $200" or "Send some money to Alice on her birthday."

Insurance: The financial market successfully facilitates risk transfer. Another person's profit is another person's hedge against his position. As previously discussed, insurance is now available through Nexus Mutual or Opyn. If you're prepared to accept a lower yield on money you've put into lending mechanisms like Compound in exchange for peace of mind, it's now possible.

Liquidity aggregation: There are numerous decentralized exchanges (DEXes) in the market, each with differing liquidity, making it difficult for customers to determine which one is ideal for their trade. With liquidity aggregators like 1inch.exchange, Paraswap, and DEX.AG that help to automatically divide orders between DEXes to assure the best possible prices, this is progressively becoming a thing of the past.

Yield optimization: Do you remember shopping around for the greatest rates on fixed deposits at various banks? In Defi, yield bouncers like idle.finance, DeFiSaver, and iEarn automatically distribute your crypto assets to the Ethereum blockchain locations with the best yield possibilities.

While there is currently no single "killer app" that bridges the user experience divide, we believe it is not far away!

Conclusion

Decentralized Finance is focused on building financial services separate from the traditional financial and political system. This would take into consideration a more open financial framework and might actually forestall precedents of censorship and discrimination from one side of the world to the other.

While an enticing thought, not all things benefit from decentralization.

Finding the use cases that are generally appropriate for the attributes of blockchains is vital in building a valuable heap of open financial products.

I want to get this information out to as many people as possible because I believe DeFi is a force that will be disrupting finance in the near future. If you enjoyed the book and found it helpful, please leave me a review. Thanks!

Metaverse For Beginners 2022

The Ultimate Guide on Investing In Metaverse, Blockchain Gaming, Virtual Lands, Augmented Reality, Virtual Reality, NFT, Real Estate, Crypto And Web 3.0

Introduction

Imagine a world where you can virtually be present at a wedding in San Francisco while you're sipping a cup of coffee in Moscow? Or a society where interacting with people is not limited to just blurry video calls and glitchy computer service.

These are the things the metaverse, the next generation of the web, intends to do. But exactly, what is this metaverse? What sets it apart from the rest of the Internet?

A Metaverse is a place where you can interact with virtual items in real-time and with real-time information. In films and shows like Iron Man, Ready Player One, Upload, and The Feed, you've probably already seen this concept being put into practice.

The Metaverse consists of three distinct components. It is first and foremost a technology that allows digital content to be placed on top of the real-world environment. In a way, this is like augmented reality (AR). Using Pokémon Go as a simplistic example, this technology can be improved in future iterations of a metaverse. It's a mix of the digital and real-world stuff. It also uses a hardware gadget to make the natural environment interactive. Using digital material, users can manipulate and interact with media displayed online. The last point includes information on anything and everything in the real world (such as an area, a shop, or a product), along with information about the user (such as the user's timetable). This data will be gleaned through the Internet and machines trained to pick up on users' habits. There are many examples of devices learning from their users' daily behaviors, like Siri (iOS) and Alexa (Android) (on Amazon).

A user's experience is enhanced by obtaining real-time information instantly and virtually through the device into the physical space. At the same time, data is being collected and applied in the background.

To better grasp the Metaverse, one can extrapolate real-world traits to an entirely virtual setting. A metaverse environment will incorporate elements of the actual world into a virtual one. A virtual London or New York, for example, may provide digital representations of real-life streets and buildings to gamers playing in a virtual gaming environment. In a virtual Apple store, you may look through and purchase digital representations of Apple products that will be shipped to your home.

This would, in many ways, represent a continuation of what we currently know as traditional e-commerce. Companies may construct metaverse worlds that not only duplicate the real-life experience but also enhance it, thanks to advances in visual technology and design capability enabled by sophisticated gaming engines like Unreal or Unity. There may be no crowd outside the Manhattan Apple store's digital counterpart at launch time.

The concept of simulating real-world settings in a virtual one is nothing new. It has been going on for a long time with concepts like second life. On the other hand, contemporary online gaming settings have shifted the Metaverse from the old-school 3D block-based worlds of the turn of the century to new, ever-evolving creative ecosystems.

User-created content is the critical difference between the metaverses of the past and today. Playing online games like Fortnite, Roblox, and Minecraft has altered our perceptions of what it means to be "online." When parents wonder why their children spend so much time in these metaverse worlds, it's not because the games or items are well-designed.

Instead, they argue that the metaverses are so compelling and well-designed in and of themselves. People participate, create, and amuse each other rather than just sitting back and watching others. People are paid to make virtual goods in Minecraft, and entire mini-industries have sprung up around them. Fortnite is a virtual stage for real-world music performers to showcase their talents. Every year, tens of millions of people participate in activities that could only occur in the Metaverse.

1.   How the Metaverse Works

Several key attributes of the metaverse are revealed by these descriptions. First of all, it will involve entering cyberspace. We will do so by using a headset such as the Oculus. Once we put our headsets on, countless universes will be at our disposal. The nature of the metaverse is still unclear since we do not know if it will be a single metaverse or a collection of multiverses. At the moment, big names in the tech industry are all working on their version of the metaverse. The most likely scenario is that users will decide which ones will become popular.

Once we enter the metaverse of our choice, virtual and augmented reality will take over. We will enter this cyberspace through an avatar. An avatar can be a representation of you or something entirely different. In either case, we can customize this avatar in any way we want. The avatar is your gateway to interacting with the virtual world. This virtual world can be anything from a classroom to moon travel. The possibilities are only limited by imagination. User-generated metaverses won't be a hot topic for the foreseeable future. However, companies that **are** creating the metaverse will surely come up with amazing concepts.

These virtual worlds will have rules of their own. Mark Zuckerberg is one of the people constantly bringing this subject up. Facebook, or Meta as it's now known, seems to have learned from its unpleasant experience with the government a few years ago. Leaving old habits, they tackle privacy, safety, and ethics with a new perspective. To ensure the metaverse is exploit-free, international NGOs have been working with the company since the beginning. In addition, Mark Zuckerberg touched on the topic in an open letter and expressed how important it is for him to create a metaverse where users are free to make their own rules. We have seen a similar approach in Web 2.0. You can befriend, unfriend, and block other users on Facebook, Slack channels are invitation-only, and your Instagram account can be private if you want. The metaverse is expected to provide all this but incorporate more policies to improve safety measures. As a result, we might not influence a metaverse, but we will control how we interact with it.

Finally, metaverses are likely to have their own economies and, in some cases, their own currencies. Metaverse transactions are expected to be made on blockchains, making cryptocurrencies and altcoins ideal tender mediums. With metaverse currencies, we will be able to rent a house, buy concert tickets, go on vacation, and pay for an online course. In addition to bringing cryptocurrencies to a whole new level, many business ideas will be generated through this system.

Right now, aside from a few examples like Decentraland, we don't have all too many real-life examples of metaverses. However, we do have some fictional examples that can be used to make the metaverse more tangible in our minds.

Metaverse in Pop Culture

Metaverses have existed as fictional concepts for decades. In fact, people like Elon Musk, Mark Zuckerberg, and other influential tech entrepreneurs are all fans of these metaverses. As software creators today, it's not uncommon for them to discuss their love of a particular franchise or book in speeches or interviews.

Star Trek, without a doubt, is one such franchise. Creator Gene Roddenberry always wowed the viewers with his vision of a better, more humane future. This is especially true for **Star Trek: The Next Generation** holodecks. Holodecks appeared in classic **Star Trek** episodes as well, but the holodeck episodes of **Star Trek: The Next Generation** are a perfect example of an early metaverse. An example of a more futuristic metaverse would be the unforgettable **Inner Light** episode. The episode depicts Captain Jean-Luc Picard living an alternate life in a capsule, only to wake up on the USS Enterprise to realize it was just an alternate life. The episode is a fan favorite, so if you're into the metaverse, you will definitely want to watch it.

The Netflix show **Black Mirror** would be a more contemporary example. The show follows a dystopian future of the metaverse, but the concepts implemented are very relevant to the core idea. Another streaming platform series about the metaverse is the Amazon Original **Upload**. Philosophical satire certainly characterizes the series, but it also explores what happens in a dystopia of free-to-play games and the current online world.

If you like fictional dystopias, a good movie depicting the metaverse is **Ready Player One**. The movie does a stellar job demonstrating how VR experiences could be in the future. Another movie that does a decent job with the mechanical side of the metaverse is **Minority Report**. Watching Tom Cruise in his prime aside, holographic images and interfaces coupled with special gloves are excellent examples of how we will navigate in the metaverse.

Another movie that is regularly brought up about the metaverse is Ironman. Tony Stark, the main character in the movie, is essentially forced to create a metaverse. He manages to create both virtual and augmented reality in the movie, which is a remarkable accomplishment and makes for a great film.

One of the best examples of how metaverses could improve the common household is **Smart House**. Our houses are already getting smart. With smart appliances connecting to devices like Alexa, we are already experiencing a tech revolution in our homes. The movie **Smart House** is an excellent example of this, delving deeply into the issue of human vs. technology, while still being entertaining.

These concepts would not exist without the development of technology. Enjoying entertainment centered around the metaverse and imagining its possibilities is both inspiring and fun. But to truly grasp the magic of the metaverse, we need to dig deep into its technological aspects. Let's examine the evolution of the internet and how we got to where we are today.

The Evolution of the Web

Tim Berners-Lee invented the 'web,' as we know it, in Switzerland in the early 1990s. We wouldn't have internet browsers until nearly half a decade later. Several years later, search engines such as Google were invented. Since then, the web and internet technologies have undergone drastic changes. Nowadays, internet use has become a survival tool for millions. There have been three major stages in the history of the internet.

The Static Web

Initially, content on the internet was predetermined. Therefore, people used the term "static web" to describe it. The concept of static content refers to any content that can be delivered to an end-user without having to be generated, modified, or processed. You could make a website, and people could browse it, but they couldn't interact with it beyond leaving a comment.

The main difference between mainstream media and Web 1.0. is user involvement in content consumption. Our lives have been forever changed by the internet because it decentralized content production. Until the internet, only a few media outlets created information, which was consumed by the masses. Having access to the internet meant that everyone could produce content. Moreover, users could influence content creation by not giving attention to the information they did not enjoy. Because of this, Web 1.0 is celebrated as the democratization of information.

Understanding the decentralization of content production is very important. This mindset later led to the decentralization of currencies and gave rise to new technologies such as Bitcoin. In other words, if you wish to achieve anything in the metaverse, just keep in mind that this internet principle always determines success in online businesses.

The Interactive Web

The democratization and decentralization of the internet eventually led to Web 2.0. In this era, people were not limited to consuming content or throwing their two cents in the comment section. With Web 2.0, they could be content creators. Wikipedia, YouTube, WordPress, and Blogger are all examples of Web 2.0's impact on the world.

Web 2.0 had a rough start with the "dot-com bubble." The dot-com bubble was a rapid increase in U.S. technology stock valuations in the late 1990s caused by investments in Web-based companies. The bubble burst in 2001, leaving Nasqad with a 77% drop and investors in a panic. Several web companies collapsed, and, for a moment, it looked like the Web was just a fad.

Obviously, this wasn't the case. Technology was advancing and growing just fine. It was the stock markets that were the problem. Amazon's Jeff Bezos is a perfect example of this. Even though Amazon lost 90% of its value during the bubble, it made its shareholders extremely wealthy, including Bezos, one of the most affluent people in the world. If a scenario like this occurs in the metaverse era, remember one thing: Long-term investors will win out as long as technology is expanding.

As a result of Web 2.0, the internet has become a sea of user-generated content. Sharing information and connecting with others has become the norm. It led to hundreds of thousands of online shops, content creation platforms, and the influencer era.

The Semantic Web
Web 3.0 is predicted to be known as the Semantic Web because it will become more intuitive for every user. The name was coined by none other than Web's original creator Tim Berners-Lee. Scientific American magazine published an article in 2001 in which Bernes-Lee outlined his vision for the internet. As an example, he presented two brothers who coordinate the logistics involved in supporting their mother's medical treatment; using intelligent agents, they execute the process automatically interacting with clinical systems, among themselves, and with their home devices.

This is the kind of intuitive technology we can expect from Web 3.0. In this third generation of the web, the goal is to provide users with a personalized experience based on their interests and needs. Amazon's Alexa, which collects information from the web and tailors it to our needs, is a prime example of Web 3.0 technologies.

Currently, we're transitioning from Web 2.0 to Web 3.0. We can expect Web 3.0 to have as significant an impact as Web 2.0 has. Web 3.0 will introduce us to many exciting new technologies, including the metaverse. In order to gain a deeper understanding of the metaverse, let's examine some of its key concepts.

2.   Virtual Reality (VR)

It is now possible for even the average user to access the world of computer graphics. This obsession with a new reality frequently begins with computer games and continues indefinitely. It allows you to perceive the world around you differently and experience things that aren't available in real life or even haven't been developed yet. Furthermore, the universe of three-dimensional graphics has no boundaries or limitations. We may create and alter it as we see fit—we can even add a fourth dimension: the measurement of our imagination. But it's never enough: people are always looking for more. Instead of just watching a visual on a monitor, they want to enter this world and engage with it. Virtual Reality is a technology that has become extremely popular and fashionable in the last decade (VR). Virtual Reality is thought to have started in the 1950s, although it was only widely used in the late 1980s and 1990s. This might be attributed to Jaron Lanier, a pioneering computer scientist with the term "virtual reality" in 1987. Virtual reality research continued throughout the 1990s, and films like The Lawnmower Man served to enhance its profile. Most virtual reality settings are primarily visual experiences displayed on a computer screen or through stereoscopic displays. Auditory stimulation via speakers or headphones may be included in virtual Reality. The virtual Environment can be interacted with using a keyboard, mouse, or wired glove. Virtual Reality's history has been chiefly one of the attempts to make an experience more authentic. Visual and, to a lesser extent, auditory examples make up the majority of historical examples. This is because vision, followed by hearing, delivers the most information of all the human senses. Visual and auditory perceptions account for roughly 90% of our overall worldview.

Evolution of Virtual Reality (VR)

Ivan Sutherland created the "make (virtual) world phrase in the original window, sounds authentic, feels real, and responds realistically to viewers' activities in 1965. It's been a long time, and many studies have been done since then. Let's peek shortly in the last three decades of study in virtual Reality and its highlights:

«   **Sensorama** –The Sensorama engine was founded in 1957 and patented in 1962 under patent # 3,050,870. Morton Heilig creates a multi-sensory simulator. Films that have been recorded in color and stereo coupled with binaural sound, aroma, wind, and vibration. This is the first approach to creating a virtual reality system and has all the features like that, but it's not interactive.

« **Display Ultimate** - in 1965, Ivan Sutherland suggested a central virtual reality solution: an artificial world construction concept that included interactive graphics, force-feedback, sound, smell, and taste.

« Damocles Sword - First Virtual Reality system is realized in hardware, not the concept. Ivan Sutherland builds a device that is considered the first appearance of the head installed (HMD), with the appropriate head tracking. It supports stereo views that are updated correctly according to the position and orientation of the user's head.

What is Virtual Reality (VR)?

The development of virtual Reality extended considerably stormier towards the 1990s, and the term "virtual reality" became extremely widespread. Virtual Reality is a term that we hear about in almost every kind of media; people use it frequently and, in many situations, incorrectly. Virtual Reality (VR) is a popular term for an immersive, interactive computer-mediated experience in which a person observes a synthetic (simulated) environment using specialized human-computer interface equipment.

It interacts with the Environment's virtual objects as if they were real. In a shared synthetic environment, like a battlefield, multiple people can see and interact with one another. A computer-generated virtual environment that a person can move through and change in real-time is called "virtual reality." The virtual Environment can be seen in the display installed in the head, computer monitor, or a large projection screen. Using head and hand tracking devices, the user can see, move about, and alter the Virtual Environment. The significant distinction between VR systems and traditional media (such as radio and television) is the virtual reality structure's three-dimensionality.

Immersion, presence, and interactivity are typical features of virtual Reality which keeps him away from other representational technology. Virtual Reality does not mimic actual Reality also does not have representative functions. Humans cannot distinguish between perceptions, hallucinations, and illusions. VR has developed into a new phase and has become a different field in computing. The VR utility has been studied in car design, robot design, chemistry, biology, education, building design and construction.

Types of Virtual Reality Systems

There are various types of virtual reality systems:

Ø Immersive system.

The highest priority is given to the immersive system. As we have mentioned, the immersive design ruled out the natural world and put humans in the world of animation that was entirely generated by the computer.

Ø   Window on World (WoW)

This is a typical virtual world developed on a desktop PC. The most common form of WOW is a computer game that uses real-world 3D simulations. Here users must peek into the virtual world using a monitor placed on the desktop.

Ø   Video Mapping

This is a technique used to map human movements using special electronic devices such as cameras. Here input to the computer is a human movement, and output is a human 2D graphics image that shows its interests.

Ø   **Telepresence**

This is another virtual reality technique where we use some remote sensors somewhere in the virtual world that maps human actions and connects them to activities that objects in the virtual world must do. Firefighters use this type of virtual reality in several critical conditions. Unique robots that are fixed with this type of sensor help them.

Ø   Mixed Reality

This is a technique that combines the system of virtual reality and telepresence. Here the input for the telepresence system and virtual Reality is given information. The fighters see the map produced by the computer and connect it to the data available with it. The surgeon correlates images taken by cat scanning and taken by the computer.

Basic Terminology and Definitions

Many people, mainly the researchers, use the word natural Environment instead of virtual reality "because of the hype and unrealistic expectations related." In addition, two essential terms must be mentioned when talking about VR: telepresence and cyberspace. They are both combined with VRs, but have a slightly different context:

- **Telepresence** – This term was created by Marvin Minsky (1980), referring to the teleoperation system for the manipulation of long-distance physical objects. This is a specific type of virtual reality that simulates a natural but long-distance environment (within a distance or scale or scale). More appropriate definitions say that telepresence occurs when "on the work site, the manipulator has the dexterity to allow operators to perform normal human functions; at the control, stationworksiterator accepts sufficient quantity and the quality of sensory feedback to provide a feeling of actual presence at work."

- **Cyberspace** –Created and defined by William Gibson as "consensual hallucinations experienced every day by billions of valid operators, graphic representations of data witnessed from each computer in the human system." Today the term virtual world is somewhat related to the entertainment system and the World Wide Web (Internet).
- **Telexistence:** This theory was first proposed by Susumu Tachi in Japan in 1980 and 1981 as a patent, and the first report was published in Japanese in 1982 and English in 1984. It allows humans to have a real-time sensation in places besides Where it exists and can interact with a distant environment, which may be accurate, virtual, or a combination of both. It also refers to the sophisticated teleoperation system that allows operators to perform small tasks with feelings in replacement robots that work in a distant environment.

- **Human-Computer Interaction (HCL)** refers to the study and processes humans interact with computers. Very basic HCI is simple like a keyboard and mouse, while HCI is sophisticated can be considered a controlled interaction between someone and a laptop. **Haptics** – The word "haptics" refers to the ability to feel a natural or synthetic mechanical environment through touch. Haptics also include Kinesthesia, the ability to understand body position, movement, and weight. • Haptics technology - provides forced feedback to users about the physical properties and movement of virtual objects represented by computers. A haptic joystick, For example, offers dynamic resistance to users based on video game actions. Haptics combines touch elements (tactile) and movement (kinesthetic). Applications that simulate physical properties such as weight, momentum, friction, texture, or haptics resistance communicate these properties through the interface, allowing users to "feel" what happens on the screen. Immersion Levels in Virtual Reality Systems

A computer generates sensory impressions given to the human senses in a virtual environment system. In Virtual Reality, the type and quality of these perceptions impact the amount of immersion and sense of presence. Ideally, information should be given to all users' minds in high-resolution, high-quality, and consistent across all screens. Furthermore, the Environment should respond realistically to the user's activities. On the other hand, the reality is significantly different from this ideal scenario. Many applications simply stimulate one or a few senses, and they frequently provide low-quality, unsynchronized data. We may categorize VR systems based on the level of immersion they provide to the user.

- **Non-Immersive (Desktop VR) systems** – Virtual desktop reality is a lower immersive level that can be easily used in many applications without special devices. Sometimes it is called a window system in the world (WOW). This is the type of most straightforward virtual reality application. VR Desktop is when computer users see a virtual environment via one or more computer screens. A user can then link with that Environment, but it is not immersed. It uses a conventional monitor to display images (generally monoscopic) in the world. There are no other sensory outputs supported. Virtual Desktop reality has begun to make its way and popularity in modern education because it provides visualization and real-time interaction in the virtual world that resembles the real world.

- **Semi-Immersive (Fish Tank VR) systems** –Enhanced VR Desktop version. This system supports head tracking and therefore increases the feeling of "being there" thanks to the effect of movement parallax. They still use conventional monitors (often with LCD shutter glasses to watch stereoscopic) but generally do not support sensory output.

- **Immersive systems** – The main version of the VR system. They let users immerse themselves in the world produced by a computer with HMD assistance that supports stereoscopic views of the scene according to the position and user orientation. This system can be increased by audio, haptic, and sensory interfaces.

Characteristics of Immersive (VR)

1) The unique characteristics of immersive virtual realities can be summarized as follows: The appearance referenced by the head provides a natural interface for navigation in three-dimensional space and allows one to look, take a walk, and the ability to fly in a virtual environment.

2) Stereoscopic viewing promotes the perception of depth and the sense of space.

3) The virtual world is presented fully and is related to human size.

4) Realistic interactions with virtual objects through data gloves and similar devices allow manipulation, operation, and virtual world control.

5) Convincing illusions to be wholly immersed in the artificial world can be increased by auditories, haptic, and other non-visual technology.

6) Networked applications allow for shared virtual environments.

v   Uses of Virtual Reality

It's difficult to define all VR applications because they have advanced far enough in numerous fields. However, some of the applications of virtual Reality are discussed below. Virtual reality software bundle EDS Jack is an example of commercially accessible virtual reality software. It is mainly utilized for research into visibility and ergonomics. These are two of the many areas where Virtual Reality may help. For example, operators value visibility and ergonomics when constructing massive mechanical equipment like a bulldozer or even an automobile.

Probably not. Would you buy a car that was difficult to drive or had poor visibility? Many businesses spend a significant amount of money improving how their products interact with operators. Building prototypes is quite expensive, costing upwards of a few million dollars for single equipment in the case of the bulldozer. The corporation could immediately examine the viability and ergonomics of their machine using virtual Reality and make modifications without ever having to spend money on developing hardware. Driving and flying simulations are other areas where Virtual Reality is widely employed. This allows users to experience driving a car while avoiding real-world punishment to make mistakes. For instance, MPI Vega Prime is a software program that can simulate any form of bullying. Within the software package, the user creates the virtual Environment. Its most significant benefit is its realistic physics engine, which allows collision detection. The most popular sort of machine simulation is flight simulators. Other instances include the employment of simulators by the US Army to train tank soldiers in virtual tank battles. NASA also uses a virtual reality simulator to instruct astronauts on land the space shuttle.

Ø Advantages

 Virtual Reality has also been utilized extensively to treat phobias (such as fear of height, fly, and spider) and post-traumatic stress disorders. This kind of therapy has proven effective in academic settings, and some commercial entities now offer them to patients. Although it was found that using a standardized patient for the training was more realistic, computer-based simulations provide several advantages over direct training. They aim to increase exposure to emergencies such as life to improve decision-making and performance and reduce psychological pressure in real health emergencies.

Ø Disadvantages

Some psychologists are worried that immersion in a virtual psychological environment can affect users. They suggest that refreshing the system that places users in a situation of violence, especially as a participant in violence, can lead to users being sensitive. As a result, there is a panic that entertainment systems can breed a sociopath generation. Involving a virtual environment has the potential to make addicted more. Another emergence of concerns involves criminal acts. Defining actions such as murder or sex crimes have been problematic in the virtual world. At which point can the authorities impose a person's fees with real crimes for actions in the virtual Environment? Studies show that people can have a natural physical and emotional reaction to stimulation in the virtual Environment, so it is possible that victims of virtual attacks can feel real emotional trauma.

3.   Augmented Reality

While virtual reality is an exclusively digital environment created by one or more computers or applications that simulate actual reality, augmented reality (AR) represents the real world enriched with virtual objects or details that lead to improving or "increasing" the experience.

It is based on the expansion or integration of the surrounding reality with computer-generated 3D graphics images, which modify the original environment without affecting interaction possibilities.

In essence, augmented reality transforms vast masses of data and analytics into images or animations, a digital level that is superimposed on the physical world by integrating with it.

What Does It Take To Create Augmented Reality?

Not being as immersive as virtual reality, it does not necessarily need specific viewers for which everyday devices such as smartphones or special screens can be used (as in the case of car accessories).

How Does Augmented Reality Work?

Augmented reality starts from a device equipped with a video camera - such as a smartphone, tablet, or smart glass - on which AR software has been loaded. When the user indicates the device at an object and looks at it, the software recognizes it through computerized vision technology, which analyzes the flow of images.

Then the device downloads the object information from the cloud, just like a browser downloads a page via the URL. The critical difference is that AR information is presented in a 3D experience superimposed on the object rather than on a two-dimensional page that appears on a screen.

What the user sees, therefore, is partly natural and partly digital. At this point, we must introduce the overlay principle: the camera reads the object in the frame, the system recognizes it. It activates a new level of communication that overlaps and integrates perfectly with reality, enhancing detailed data about that object.

Headsets are the critical technology for both virtual and augmented reality. It is, thus, not unexpected that some of the best-known names in the traditional IT market have thrown themselves into the construction of this equipment which, depending on the model, can be destined for different types of uses (gaming and more).

Google Glass is a trademark of smart glasses developed by the Mountain View company, a pair of glasses equipped with augmented reality through which you can access various information:

you can read websites and news online, check social networks, view maps and driving directions through Google Maps, participate in video conferences, take photos and shoot videos, all without the use of hands (hands-free). Perhaps due to the too-high price, probably because it arrived too early (with the official debut in mid-2014), Google Glass had a reasonably tepid welcome from ordinary consumers, also for issues related to usability, as well as protection of privacy. Google, therefore, withdrew the product from sale, which - despite some relaunch rumors - has never seen the light again.

Augmented And Virtual Reality Viewers

The Oculus Rift, produced by the company of the same name then acquired by Facebook, which, starting from 2016, has quickly established itself as one of the most popular virtual reality viewers for gaming, has been decidedly more fortunate. To contend with the priority, there are other viewers produced by names such as Samsung (with its Gear VR), which needs the latest generation smartphone to work and which is to be inserted inside the mask of the viewer, and Huawei with VR2 (first model released in 2016 and then updated in 2018) which can be connected to a PC to use it with games designed for machines with higher computing power than the integrated one.

Mixed Reality Viewer

In the business field, however, at least for the moment, Microsoft's Hololens (created in 2015 and updated in 2019) has captured the most interest, a viewer for mixed reality, specifically designed to bring value to enterprise projects, i.e., in all those work processes that can benefit from a minimum of digital interaction and in which there is a need to experiment with something new.

Growth Market With Ar In The Lead

The global VR and AR market reached a value of $6.158 billion in 2017 and is expected to travel at a growth rate of 58.1% between now and 2023. The growing penetration of smartphones, along with advances, will drive the market in connectivity and information technology, in addition to the significant investments and innovations conducted by technology giants such as Apple, Google, and Facebook, including tools, platforms, and services.

Virtual reality accounts for about 60% of the total turnover, but by 2023 things should be reversed: AR will travel at a development rate of 73.8%, higher than virtual reality. The demand for sectors such as tourism and retail should be driving AR. According to analyses by Statista, IDC, and Goldman Sachs, by 2020, more than 1 billion users will use AR applications and services, helping to fuel a market that is estimated to exceed $215 billion within two / three years.

A parallel statement can be created for the hardware-software division: at the moment, about 65% of the sector's turnover is the prerogative of hardware devices, such as virtual reality viewers. But the demand for software solutions is set to travel faster, approaching these percentages. The USA, which represents the dominant country of this new market, is destined to maintain this leadership position in the following four years, even if Canada, Central Eastern Europe, and Western Europe will experience higher rates of development.

Despite analysts making market growth estimates by unifying virtual reality and augmented reality, developers believe that augmented reality will drive the growth trends of the next few years: "where virtual reality reproduces the real world to create spaces digitally, augmented reality understands and includes the real world; AR superimposes virtual images on real environments, spaces, and images, creating a potential for customer experiences that are very different from those possible with VR," Digital Trends reports.

VR environments, by their nature, require the utmost attention from the user (who is immersed in a reconstructed environment within which he can move and interact only "digitally"), which makes the technology inadequate for real social interaction outside of a digital world.

Instead, AR makes it possible (and this is precisely where its strength lies) because it has the potential to act as an on-demand "co-pilot" in everyday life, integrating perfectly into the daily interactions that users have in the real world.

Interactions that can range from gaming to entertainment, from sports to the shopping experience, up to coming into play in business and work contexts: 64% of American consumers in the United States, even believe that augmented reality will bring benefits to the workplace, for example by facilitating collaboration between teams located in different locations or by accelerating design and innovation processes.

Companies are also in favor of these situations. That is confirmed by research recently carried out by Capgemini entitled "Augmented and Virtual Reality in Operations: A guide for investment," conducted on about 700 executives in the automotive, manufacturing, and utility sectors.

82% of companies currently implementing these solutions believe the benefits exceed their expectations. In comparison, a good 46% of respondents expect AR and VR to become mainstream within the next three years, while a further 38% expect this transition within the next three to five years.

In general, augmented reality is considered more applicable in the company by supporting a more splendid series of innovative uses precisely because of its ability to interact with reality. Some virtual reality solutions are considered capable of positively impacting businesses.

45% of companies use AR, while the percentage drops to 36% for companies that have implemented virtual reality (the rest are still in the experimental phase).

The extent of the investments and the areas of application of augmented reality

When Augmented Reality Began: Origins And Evolutionary Scenarios

The first condition of augmented reality dates back to 1968 when Ivan Sutherland developed the first AR glasses. Also, in the same year, the origin of the first VR viewer can be traced back when Ivan Sutherland, together with Bob Sproull, developed a primitive solution with wireframe graphics similar in design to the cumbersome mechanical machinery called Sensorama of 1962, the earliest known example of immersive multisensory technology by Morton Helig.

In the 90s, virtual time reality was coined by Jaron Lanier so that an organized vision of how portable devices, the Internet, and GPS can come together to give life to devices capable of increasing or enriching the level of information in the real world.

Even if the first projects were not very successful, in those years, the foundations were laid that allowed:

in 2015 to see tools such as Samsung Gear VR, Google Cardboard, and Oculus Rift on the market, technologies that will enable us to be catapulted into another world, into another room, into an environment different from the one in which we are physical;

in 2016 to witness the mass diffusion of AR, mainly thanks to the Pokémon Go game, which allowed us to understand the novelty and the difference with VR: bringing digital content simply and immediately into the physical world.

However, the phenomenon has exploded in recent years and has turned the spotlight on the new big trend, Mixed Reality (MR). Defined by analysts as the combination of virtual reality and augmented reality aimed at producing new settings and visualizations where digital and physical objects coexist and interact in real-time, Mixed Reality has a market that:

will arrive in 2024 to generate a turnover that will touch 6.86 billion dollars (according to analysts of Grand View Research).

Much more technologically advanced than VR (because it combines the use of different technologies, sensors, wearable devices, very advanced optics, and ever-greater computing power for data analysis), Mixed Reality allows you to raise AR to a superior experience enabling people to experience increasingly vast, realistic scenarios within spaces and times that become unlimited.

Giants such as Facebook, Samsung, Sony, and Nintendo are not the only ones to invest in AR-VR technologies, given that even the panorama of startups dedicated to this area is gradually expanding.

A lot is being supported in AR and VR. The application frontiers are comprehensive. Soon, there will be business opportunities in many areas, from the world of gaming to events, from health to insurance through Retail, Education, Sport, and Live Entertainment.

Augmented Reality In Marketing

Augmented reality is, in fact, a form of visual content management 2.0 that allows companies and organizations to engage customers through innovative ways: in fact, it adds new levels of information in real-time and with a high rate of interaction using mobile devices of any type, including wearable technologies.

Not surprisingly, the first experiments were in entertainment, exploiting that effect capable of capturing attention through surprise and virtual magic, making the experience with the brand as immersive and engaging as possible.

Exclusivity, personalization, and uniqueness are advantages of integrating augmented and virtual reality into the broader customer experience strategies to allow consumers to interact with the brand in a new way. People love to feel special in the eyes of brands and appreciate exclusive services; whether it's an app that allows them to try out new furniture in the apartment they live in, or that offers tips for the perfect makeup based on their skin type, the important thing is that they are personalized.

4.Stocks In The Metaverse That You Should Consider Buying

The metaverse, described as immersive and interactive virtual online environments, has piqued the interest of the investing and business worlds in recent months. As a result, companies of all kinds are pouring billions of dollars into attempting to capitalize on the internet's next big thing. This comprises Facebook, Oculus, Instagram, and WhatsApp's parent company, Meta Platforms (NASDAQ: FB). The IT behemoth intends to spend more than $10 billion each year on metaverse investments.

However, Meta isn't the only firm working on the metaverse. To ride this long-term trend, here are three metaverse stocks to invest in right now.

1. Match Group

The online dating business is dominated by Match Group (NASDAQ: MTCH). It owns several applications and services; the most well-known of which is Tinder, the most widely used mobile dating app globally. Subscription or a la carte sales currently account for most of the company's revenue. They give users access to more services and put their dating profiles in front of more potential matches. In the most recent quarter, Match Group's paying users climbed 16 percent year over year to 16.3 million, suggesting that 16.3 million people spent money on the company's various services.

This technique has proven successful so far, and it should continue to do so in the coming years. On the other hand, Match Group has stated its intention to make its services even more immersive over the next decade in its most recent shareholder letter. This will begin with video capabilities, which Match Group has already included in a number of its offerings. For example, tinder has just unveiled a "explore" area where users may connect based on the same interests or activities. In addition, it intends to introduce a virtual currency on a global scale to make purchasing virtual goods and services on the platform easier.

Match Group's most ambitious project outside of Tinder is Single Town in South Korea, administered by its latest acquisition Hyperconnect. Single Town is an experimental virtual world where singles may meet up and converse/hang out in a virtual setting utilizing avatars. Although the concept is novel and unlikely to catch on, it reflects Match Group's dedication to enhancing the services it owns.

2. Take-Two Interactive

Take-Two Interactive (NASDAQ: TTWO) is a video game developer and publisher known for titles such as (GTA) Grand Theft Auto, Red Dead Redemption, and NBA 2K. GTA, its most metaverse-like franchise, is its main revenue generator. To put things in perspective, Take-most Two's recent premium GTA game was GTA V, released in 2013. It was one of the most popular games last decade, and it continues to be a major revenue generator for the corporation.

What gives that this is possible? Take-Two Interactive published GTA Online simultaneously as GTA V. GTA Online is a virtual environment set in the fictional Southern California metropolis of San Andreas. Take-Two has consistently released upgrades and expansions for the GTA Online community since its launch, and they have fueled spending on virtual goods and services. GTA Online is probably the best example of a living metaverse in operation right now, while not as immersive as virtual reality headsets (at least not yet).

GTA Online will be released as a standalone game in March 2022 to increase the number of individuals who can interact in the virtual world. GTA VI's final release, whenever that may be, will almost certainly result in even more recurring interaction in the GTA Online universe. GTA Online will undoubtedly get more immersive as the virtual world becomes more immersive in the future decade, benefiting any Take-Two Interactive owners.

3. Roblox

Another metaverse stock is Roblox (NYSE: RBLX); however, it "flips the script" compared to Match Group and Take-Two Interactive. Rather than creating its own metaverse-like experiences, Roblox provides the tools for other developers to create their virtual worlds for users. Consider it the YouTube of video games and virtual world creation.

The bulk of Roblox's users are under 18; hence the platform's experiences are mostly geared at children. However, the business believes that with time, it will be able to improve its graphics production tools to bring its games closer to those released by professional studios such as Take-Two. With 47.3 million daily active users (DAUs) after the third quarter, Roblox is already a massive online community. These customers are splurging on Robux, the platform's in-game currency that developers can utilize to offer in-game experiences or things. (Roblox profits by taking a percentage of each transaction.)

Roblox's net bookings (their sales measure) reached $637.8 million in the third quarter, generating $170.6 million in free cash flow. As previously said, the platform is now geared at children, while Roblox is working on one of the most pure-play metaverse systems in the world. As a result, Roblox might be a terrific long-term compounder for your portfolio if you believe the trend toward increasingly immersive and virtual worlds will continue in the next decades.

10 stocks we like better than Match Group

When our award-winning expert team has a stock suggestion, it pays to pay attention. After all, the Motley Fool Stock Advisor newsletter, which they've been publishing for almost a decade, has tripled the market.

They have announced their top 10 stocks for investors to buy right now... and Match Group wasn't one of them! Yes, they believe these ten stocks are even better bargains.

Virtual Real Estate Investing

Virtual real estate investing is often considered the domain of more experienced real estate investors. This isn't entirely correct, though. With the influence of the coronavirus on the US real estate market, virtual real estate investing is here to stay. You do not need to go to other states to conduct property research. In addition, purchasing an investment property is no longer restricted by location. Anyone from anywhere may make profitable investment selections thanks to real estate investment tools and real estate investor websites.

What Is Virtual Real Estate Investing?

Virtual real estate investing is conducting property research and investment property analysis utilizing real estate investment software before purchasing an investment property. It's essentially remote real estate investing instead of the traditional method of physically attending showings. It is a cost-effective option to perform out-of-state real estate investing because it eliminates the need for travel and the costs and time connected with it. Not to add, it simplifies the process of scouting for off-market properties, which often includes physically driving around neighborhoods. Long-distance real estate investing can be done from the comfort of one's own home by virtual real estate investors.

How to Get Started in Virtual Real Estate Investing

It does not have to be difficult to become a real estate investor. You can even start it as a side venture for passive income if you have the necessary real estate resources. However, because you are no longer bound to your city, virtual real estate investing gives up a lot of alternatives for any budget and investment goals. Purchasing rental property outside of your state may be more profitable for you. So, if you're ready to put this method to work for you, here's how to get started:

How to Choose a Real Estate Market

Long-distance real estate investing can be perplexing at first since there are so many options to consider. If you don't know where to begin, pick a state that interests you. It might be a state with favorable Airbnb regulations or ideal for a holiday property. It might also be a property with no rent control and a large population if you're trying to go into typical rental rentals. Then decide whether cities or towns within it could be of interest to long-term tenants or tourists. How did you figure that out? There will be visitors if there are tourist attractions, sites, or natural features nearby. To see if there will be a demand for long-term rental homes, you can look into market statistics online, such as the number of renters, the price-to-rent ratio, and the state of the job market and economy.

This stage, even with a little research, can be challenging. That is why virtual real estate investing requires real estate investment instruments. You can't know what's happening in every town's housing market, but real estate investment software like Mashvisor can. It gathers information from various listing sites to almost automate your real estate market research. Mashvisor's real estate heatmap allows you to explore neighborhoods in any city in the United States. Different types of neighborhood data can be used to do analysis:

- Traditional and Airbnb rental income

- Listing price

- Airbnb occupancy rate

- The average rate of return on a rental property (in the form of traditional and Airbnb cash on cash return)

In this manner, you can quickly learn about the housing market in the area of your choice and determine whether it is a good place to invest in real estate. In addition, it gives you a graphic representation of the real estate market study. The heatmap allows you to search for items based on essential parameters, such as cash on cash return. The map is filtered, and the corresponding neighborhoods are highlighted in green with high values. You don't need to have ever visited the location to use this data – virtual real estate investing means you know more about the investment potential than the locals.

Making a Business Decision

Buying a rental property out of state and investing close to home have one thing in common: you must conduct an investment property study before selecting a property for sale in either scenario. This entails delving deeper into a property's financials and determining if it would be a lucrative investment. Mashvisor can assist traditional and virtual real estate investors with this. The platform does this analysis is done for you by the platform, which allows you to compare alternative options. Here's a quick rundown of what the automatic analysis includes:

Expenses and possible funding sources To calculate expenditures and return on investment, enter your mortgage or cash data into the investment property calculator. Utilities, insurance, property management fees, and HOA fees are all estimated based on historic property data for the locality. As a result, you can immediately see if a certain investment property for sale is a good fit for your real estate investing plan.

This is a rental scheme. Rental income, cash flow, cap rate, cash on cash return, monthly expenses, and occupancy rate are all reported by Mashvisor. In addition, you'll get a handy side-by-side comparison of Airbnb vs. traditional renting to help you decide which rental plan is the most profitable.

The Investment Property Calculator on Mashvisor

Investigate the competition. Mashvisor lists similar rental homes in the neighborhood to make out-of-state real estate investing even easier. In addition, both standard and Airbnb rental comps are available. Size, occupancy rate, and, for Airbnbs, the Airbnb nightly rate, as well as Airbnb ratings and reviews, are all available. As a result, you'll be able to set a reasonable rental charge.

Mashvisor's Rental Comps

You can finish the sale remotely with some assistance once you've discovered your ideal investment property. In most regions, you may engage a home inspection service to visit the property without you and give you peace of mind. Then, to work on the discussions and the offer, it would be beneficial to contact a local agency. This can be done quickly over the phone or via email (listings on Mashvisor give all agents' contact details). Finally, a digital signature is required. Many documents must be signed before the transaction can be completed, not to mention leases once you have taken ownership. Most counties now accept digitally signed documents, which will save you a lot of paperwork. After all, virtual real estate investing is technologically advanced and shouldn't have a lot of paperwork.

Metaverse Virtual Real Estate Is Booming.

The Sandbox, one such virtual world, is now topping the pack in terms of traders and sales. Last week, the Sandbox had the biggest trading volume, with more than $86 million traded for land plot NFTs, while Decentraland came in second with more than $15 million traded for land plot NFTs.

What, then, is the growing appeal of purchasing a virtual parcel of land?

NFTs and play-to-earn games, such as Axie Infinity by Vietnamese studio Sky Mavis, have introduced an entire generation of individuals into shared online communities, according to Hayden Hughes, CEO of crypto social trading platform Alpha Impact. Hughes stated that when these communities grow, members have a creative drive to express themselves by owning assets in the metaverse, such as land.

"Creatives who sincerely want to express themselves, as well as speculators looking to profit, are driving the rush to acquire land in the metaverse. Unlike the 2017 ICO [initial coin offering] bubble, the metaverse has widespread adoption and a vibrant (though early) ecosystem. "Facebook / Meta isn't the market leader in this field, and the rebrand has drawn attention to the ecosystem," Hughes explained.

Not only is the demand for metaverse experiences growing, but so is the price of metaverse land, according to DappRadar. Last week, metaverse land plot NFTs in various virtual worlds accounted for five of the ten most expensive NFT transactions.

According to the data, the top grosser was the Fashion Street Estate in Decentraland, which changed hands for 618.000 MANA, or $2.42 million. However, an Axie Genesis plot – the most valuable territory in yet another stand-alone metaverse game – sold for 550 Ethereum last month (ETH). According to a tweet from the creators, this purchase was "the greatest sale ever for a single piece of digital property," with 550 ETH worth $2.48 million as of Dec. 3.

Axie Infinity, Denctraland, and Metaverse Gaming are just a few of the games available.

"Lunacia, the Axie motherland, is divided into tokenized parcels of land that operate as residences and bases of action for its Axies," according to the Axie Infinity whitepaper. Plots can be improved over time with a range of resources and crafting ingredients gathered throughout the game."

According to the developer whitepaper, Lunacia comprises 90,601 plots of land that are represented as NFTs and can be freely sold by users. However, the Genesis property in question is highly valuable due to its scarcity: the game's 90,601 plots contain only 220 Genesis plots.

This expansion of the "creative economy," also known as "play-to-earn," allows users to own their digital assets as NFTs, exchange them with others in the game, and occasionally transport them to other digital experiences, according to recent research from Grayscale Investments. As a result, projects like Decentraland are constructing an open-world metaverse in which users can log in to play games and earn MANA (Decentraland's native currency), which can be used to buy NFTs like as LAND or collectibles), vote on economic governance, or build NFTs. In addition, this architecture provides users with significant interoperability between systems as a value proposition for their time spent in-game.

Land in the metaverse, according to Matt Maximo, research analyst at Grayscale Investments and co-author of the report, is a fascinating concept because traditional real estate is valued largely based on proximity to shops, services, and other people – you're limited by the time it takes to travel from your home.

Players in several metaverses, such as Decentraland, can teleport worldwide, making travel quick and unrelated to valuation. Given the developing nature of the market, many of the higher-priced sales have come from LAND lots in desirable locations, such as proximity to prominent metaverse attractions.

"Investing in LAND is exciting, but it carries the same risks as any other emerging market." LAND and MANA owners are motivated to keep the Decentraland map small and maintain the number of parcels low, but "there will come a time where enlarging the map and producing more LAND to sell will benefit them more than the dilution of their property," he explained.

He went on to say that because LAND plots are non-fungible tokens, liquidity is considerably lower than with the underlying tokens like MANA.

"If you're in a hurry to sell, you can be compelled to sell below market value to the highest bidder, whereas if I have MANA, I can go to an exchange like Uniswap or Coinbase and make the sale instantaneously," he added.

In the Metaverse, Is There an Infinite Land?

While the metaverse's rising options have greatly incentivized property purchase as a way for players to stake their claim in a virtual environment, one potential difficulty is that land may be in limitless supply.

"As a result, it's difficult to predict how much land will be worth in the future, and buying today could be considered a dangerous investment." If digital land, for example, becomes oversupplied, supply-demand economics kicks in, and the price drops. However, for investors who wish to be among the first to own land in the digital world, the sheer amount of possibilities that the metaverse may be able to offer may outweigh the danger." BLOCKv & SmartMedia Technologies co-founder Reeve Collins told GOBankingRates.

According to Eduardo Erlo, marketing manager of blockchain-based encrypted messenger Status, the frenzy of buying digital real estate could lead to a temporary slump. Erlo went on to say that because land in the metaverse is eternally abundant, paying a lot of money for it now might be a waste of money.

He said that one way to get around the endless abundance of digital land would be for some metaverses to have built-in scarcity regarding plots of land — such as the Genesis virtual land discussed earlier — similar to the built-in monetary investment scarcity offered by Bitcoin. "It's still too early to know anything about all of this," he said, "but it's interesting to watch."

According to Grayscale, the commercial opportunity for bringing any number of metaverses to life might be worth more than $1 trillion in yearly income. In addition, revenue from virtual game worlds might climb to $400 billion in 2025, up from $180 billion in 2020.

Purchases of virtual land in the metaverse, according to several experts, can be considered an investment. According to Robert Powers, director of decentralized media at Vivid Labs, the metaverse — and the many metaverses within it — will deliver on promises and change into a dynamic virtual environment in which we will all be contributing in some manner.

However, Powers told GOBankingRates that we are still in the early days of the emerging metaverse — or metaverses because there will likely be many, not just one — and that we should be wary of speculation that leads to the kind of rapid price increases that we are seeing right now in the digital land market.

"However, this burst of innovation gives immense promise for what's to come in a more completely immersive digital environment." "Perhaps these early digital land buyers are the digital equivalents of owning the Empire State Building or New York City itself," he speculated.

Another point about the value of digital real estate is made by Dan Patterson, general partner at Sfermion, an NFT-focused investment business.

5.   Payment in the Metaverse

Role of Payment in the Metaverse

Payment is described as support for online payment systems, platforms, and activities. It is the legal cash and digital currency exchange, currency trading, financial services like Bitcoin and Ethereum, and other blockchain technology. Metaverse payment will be made possible by the existence of both legal and digital currencies. Based on China's present regulatory rules for digital currencies such as Bitcoin, the conflict between centralized and decentralized money will remain in the Metaverse.

Payment comprises the recognition of persons and brands, the evaluation of products or services, and the agreement on transaction details to grasp the most fundamental logic of payment.

Recognition of Individuals and Corporations

Payment is made with cards and mobile phones in the physical world, while authentication is done with passwords, biometric data, and other techniques. People keep their unique serial numbers on a secure carrier. We must investigate what constitutes a secure carrier in the metaverse. Integrating SE security chips to every metaverse device, like virtual reality headsets with SE security chips, turns it into a carrier carrying payments under the existing security route. However, the metaverse's unique identifying code for users and businesses has many possibilities, like the latest fire non-fungible token technology.

The Process of Determining Goods or Services

In the Metaverse, goods and services become digital, such as in games. If a product can alter information with easy copy, paste, and delete, and its worth fluctuates dramatically in a short period, the transaction has major flaws. This problem can be better solved using blockchain technology and NFT technologies.

Consensus on Transaction Records

According to the conventional online payment concept, the account owner will rule the world, and the likelihood still applies to the Metaverse. If there is identity verification, the accounting system will have a functioning space. It has to function similarly to the present e-commerce system's role or method so that both entities are comfortable with the transaction's substance, which the blockchain network's consensus system can do.

Preparation for Payment Companies

Meta announced the crypto initiative in Libra in 2019. The giants were already studying the payment systems required by the Metaverse before the metaverse buzz. Libra hopes to be a new decentralized blockchain network, low-volatility crypto, and smart contract system to provide a new avenue for credible financial service innovation. Libra is the keeper of a "basket of currencies" made up of international legal currencies, sometimes known as "stable currencies."

Participating institutions started to withdraw because of the multi-national compliance challenges. Therefore, Libra was rebranded Diem and focused on the US dollar stable currency. Furthermore, Meta is actively marketing the digital currency wallet concept, and its Novi division just conducted a small-scale experiment.

After being rebranded as Meta, it can securely manage payment channels and establish a solid basis for its metaverse plan's growth with the support of its crypto project structure. Domestic enterprises have not developed preparations for Bitcoin projects in advance due to governmental constraints, but there have been efforts to support virtual reality scenarios.

Alipay debuted VR Pay in 2016. The user places an order by selecting the product on the smartphone VR platform or VR App, confirming the purchase, entering the payment link, selecting Alipay, and clicking to complete the payment.

Finance and Payment in the Metaverse
In principle, Alipay's VR Pay continues the scheme based on Alipay's account framework. It is still a digital payment that falls within the e-commerce payment class. Furthermore, several banks use VR technology to enhance the customer experience.

Many banks, like Industrial and Commercial Bank of China, Bank of China, and Hua Xia Bank, presented virtual reality equipment during the 2016 China International Finance Exhibition to give consumers a fresh financial service experience. The Guangdong branch of China Construction Bank finished the design of the "Golden Bee" maker space in 2016. Through a 6-and-a-half-minute virtual reality experience video, the Guangdong Branch of China Construction Bank and Heixia.com partnered to develop the VR experience. The potential use case of virtual reality systems in customer experience, financial transactions, scene presentation, and other areas was discussed. Guangzhou Rural Commercial Bank put up a virtual reality business hall at the 6**th** China (Guangzhou) International Financial Exchange Expo, where clients may explore information and do self-service purchasing.

Nevertheless, at the time, banks' understanding of virtual reality was still limited, and most employed virtual reality technology to deliver information. Therefore, it fell short of the current Metaverse interoperability. Exploring how to locate situations and give services in the Metaverse will become a popular issue for financial institutions in the nearest future.

Unsolved Problems

Payments in the Metaverse may get more difficult in the future. For instance, consider the present game sector. The pricing of the same game varies according to the console platform, as does the division situation. Accounting needs vary depending on the platform sharing method, copyright, suppliers, and so forth.

There will be exchange rate issues if Metaverse has cross-border transactions paid in regular legal tender. SWIFT has introduced many initiatives to increase the ease of cross-border transactions, including GPI and SWIFT Go. Furthermore, the Group of Twenty (G20) has struck a deal and introduced the "G20 Roadmap on Strengthening Cross-Border Payments," which includes development ideas to enhance the ease of global cross-border transactions clearly and concisely to benefit Metaverse's development.

Furthermore, Chinese authorities are presently focusing on ethics' largely unnoticed issue. The financial and payment demands in the virtual world will eventually expand as the Metaverse grows in popularity. The Metaverse exists in parallel to the physical world, yet it is linked to it, and there are numerous options. This is the issue.

For example, suppose a woman uses a smart sex gadget. In that case, a hacker accesses the device, gains authorization to use the sex device, and issues a command to harm the woman severely. Will this be investigated as a case of rape? Another example is a user who acquires device rights remotely by paying a charge and instructing whether he is accused of prostitution with a woman's agreement.

Furthermore, there may be inconsistencies between digital currency and the Metaverse's physical financial system. The digital currency in the game can be used to purchase a variety of digital products in the game environment. Once a game's impact has grown sufficiently, its game props and currency will be rooted in value with physical currency, like a rare tool or a skin valued at thousands of Renminbi. The digital currency in the game and the physical currency have an exchange rate.

The Metaverse is no different. Virtual products have a specific worth if a virtual environment has enough impact and consumes enough user time. The most straightforward example is that Q coins will be able to buy buns in the future, and game coins will refuel. There is a financial oversight issue. However, a decentralized virtual currency with virtual props and impossible to monitor supervision will significantly influence the present financial system.

Need for Blockchain Payment System

Matthew Ball's Metaverse framework addressed the payment difficulty as the most difficult so far. According to him, the payment choices are so inefficient, unjust, and authoritarian. So, we may never have a Metaverse we expected until we transition to a blockchain-based system, which has its own set of issues.

Transaction fees and time delays are inherent in the current traditional payment systems. Virtual environment-based payment systems are considerably more expensive and inefficient built on these payment mechanisms. Similarly, distribution networks (consoles, Apple, etc.) lock in customers and developers by imposing hefty fees on the latter and excluding payment rivals.

Because mobile is so prevalent and vital for mass-market development, existing metaverse platforms end up paying Apple and Google Play the majority of their revenue. However, their drawbacks are mostly decentralized, which renders them inefficient and costly energy. For example, although Roblox's income-sharing agreement is tough for its creators, Apple takes a large blow itself. Blockchain and non-fungible tokens offer a potential fix and alternative to all of this.

Because of these flaws, practically all non-fungible token platforms save as much data as they could on centralized databases instead of the blockchain network. Non-fungible tokens rely on vulnerable "pointers" that might go offline at any time. Given this, it is unsurprising that some people consider the blockchain a major drawback. Do not forget that the virtual economy currently produces over $50 billion yearly and encompasses hundreds of billions of hours of use—all without using cryptocurrency or blockchain technology.

Blockchain-based payment methods for the Metaverse have some promise. However, most current ones place the blockchain cart ahead of the digital world horse.

The recent $150,000 purchase of a CryptoPunk NFT by Visa might be the first evidence that these limited-edition digital assets are being treated seriously for commerce. Until recently, the selling of these "non-fungible" assets has been connected with a high-priced piece of art, but Visa's acquisition, although also about art, is mostly about demonstrating Visa's competence in the field of employing non-fungible tokens for commerce to firms. Indeed, Visa has a future goal, according to a study released in conjunction with the CryptoPunk purchase.

Alethea AI that claims to have invented the world's pioneer "intelligent NFT," recently secured US$16 million in investment to construct a metaverse occupied with its avatars, and it is along similar lines in terms of the larger metaverse's potential, paired with the crucial function of NFTs. The talking, intelligent NFTs (iNFTs) produced by Alethea, which can conduct human-like dialogues, will populate the Metaverse.

Supporters of a completely decentralized Metaverse, in which non-fungible tokens play a key role in supporting the DeFi required for this meta-project to exist, convened recently in Paris for the Ethereum event EthCC. The importance of permissionless, trustless financial services with a high transaction rate for a Metaverse to function effectively was discussed by key speaker Ben Lakoff, co-founder of NFT-protocol Charged Particles. The Metaverse would also demand the storage and inalterability of a significant quantity of data, where blockchain technology comes into play.

Aside from the technological limitations of a space capable of supporting thousands, if not millions, of individuals online in the same virtual environment at the same time, one thing is certain: A DeFi financial design involving non-fungible tokens, which you might call the "MetaverseFi," is likely to be critical to its success.

Clearly, any major actors in the Metaverse, such as Meta and Epic Games, will have to comply with the upcoming DeFi cryptocurrency laws when developing decentralized payment systems in the metaverse.

Outlier Venture, a UK blockchain VC firm, discovered that a cryptocurrency-decentralized core is essential for a metaverse's success:

> "It requires its own economy and native currencies, where value can be earned, spent, lent, borrowed, or invested interchangeably in both a physical and virtual world, and most importantly without the intervention of a governing system."

Although the Metaverse may be virtual, I think its usage of non-fungible tokens and decentralized finance to bring it to life is solidly grounded in reality.

6.   How Will NFTs Affect The Metaverse?

NFTs can potentially upend the conventional social network paradigm of user contact, socialising, and transaction in the metaverse by upsetting the existing social network paradigm. Learn how non-fibre technologies (NFTs) might cause havoc in the digital world.

An Open And Fair Economy

At the moment, people and companies may transfer their real-world assets and services to a virtual decentralized environment called the metaverse, a virtual decentralized environment. One method of bringing more real-world assets into the metaverse is using novel gaming models in conjunction with interoperable blockchain games.

Play-to-earn gaming models are one such way that engages players in blockchain games and allows them to do more with their time. NFTs enable users to participate in financial in-game economies in the metaverse and get incentives in exchange for the value that they provide, allowing them to make money while they play. In the metaverse, play-to-earn games are also fair since participants retain complete ownership of their assets rather than having their assets owned by a single game entity, as is the case with most conventional games.

When it comes to taking part in these virtual financial in-game economies, Binance NFT's IGO launches provide a range of in-game assets from gaming projects that players may gather and integrate into a variety of virtual financial in-game economies for usage. Such in-game NFTs are in great demand, as seen by the reaction to IGO debuts, when all NFTs were sold out within minutes of the game's official launch. Axie Infinite (AXS), My Neighbor Alice (Alice), and many other popular play-to-earn games are instances of this kind of game.

On addition, gaming guilds that specialise in play-to-earn gaming will be important in increasing the overall appeal of this kind of gaming. As facilitating middlemen, guilds purchase in-game NFT resources like as land and assets, then lend them out to players who wish to utilise them in their separate virtual worlds to earn returns on their investments. Guilds that encourage players to play for money then take a tiny percentage of the money earned.

This helps foster an open and fair economy by allowing players who do not have the necessary funds to begin playing via guilds, which gives them an advantage. Players of all skill levels may benefit from guilds because they reduce the entrance barrier to play-to-earn games and make it more equitable for everyone to have a chance to participate in the metaverse economy. Briefly stated, guilds assist to jumpstart virtual economies in the metaverse by making NFT resources more available to all players.

YGG (Yield Guild Games) is an example of this, as they construct a worldwide community of metaverse players that contribute to the virtual worlds to receive in-world benefits, generating cash via the rental or sale of YGG-owned assets for a profit.

Because users may trade their NFT assets, such as in-game assets and digital real estate, on NFT markets such as Binance NFT, in-world assets can demand real-world value as well as virtual currency value. Because of their use in certain modules of the metaverse, the economic worth of NFTs delivered in-game may be determined. This provides users with the flexibility to pick the sort of material they wish to develop, such as popular assets that appeal to a wide range of consumers, original digital artwork, or specialised NFTs that confer certain skills and appearances in games to players.

Metaverses create an open and fair economy that is supported by the intrinsic qualities of the blockchain, such as immutability and transparency. Furthermore, prices are determined by the basic rule of supply and demand, based on the scarcity and on-chain value of an NFT according to its application, preventing the potential of pumping and fake value inflation.

The gaming drops offered by Binance NFT are an example of the facilitated style of operation available in the metaverse economy.

The weekly IGO releases include fundamental in-game materials from gaming projects, allowing players to get a head start early in the game in the NFT gaming sector. Aside from that, Mystery Boxes drops are only available in play-to-earn games and contain a variety of valuable items.

In addition, users may find and trade NFT products obtained in-game on the Binance NFT secondary marketplace. To assist NFT newcomers in getting started on the marketplace, Binance NFT curates a daily list of suggestions for NFT collections and creators that can be seen on the homepage, as well as rating boards that highlight the most popular NFT sales, collections, and creators.

An Extension of Identity, Community And Social Experiences

In metaverses, NFTs will also play an important part in the formation of identity, the formation of communities, and the formation of social experiences. The possession of specific NFT assets might indicate a user's support for a project or express viewpoints on the virtual and real worlds to other users. This enables like-minded people who have such NFTs to form groups to exchange experiences and generate material. The NFT avatars that are now trendy are an example of such NFTs.

A player's actual or imagined self is represented by their NFT avatar. In the metaverse, players may use their NFT avatars as access tokens, allowing them to enter and bounce between various regions. As a result, NFT avatars serve as an extension of our real-life identities, allowing us to curate and construct our virtual identities in the metaverse while maintaining complete ownership and control over our virtual identities.

Owning avatar NFTs entitles you to virtual membership in a plethora of unique experiences in both the metaverse and the actual world, hence improving your sense of belonging and social interaction. Already, NFT avatars are assisting in shaping the experiences and surroundings of the metaverses via content production and the development of new businesses and organisations.

The Bored Ape Yacht Club and CryptoPunks collections, for example, are vibrant instances of identity-shaping avatars that provide their proprietors special privileges and access to gated communities of rich people with protected material and even offline private events. Exclusive events with entry fees linked with NFTs draw attention to NFTs' function as value carriers that bridge the gap between the digital and physical worlds.

To find and acquire NFT avatars, you may go to the Binance NFT Marketplace, which offers a wide range of inexpensive NFT avatar options to choose from.

Property Ownership: Virtual Real Estate

Through the usage of NFTs, people may claim complete ownership of their virtual lands and spaces in the virtual world. The blockchain technology that underpins the asset allows users to show ownership of the asset and build their virtual real estate as they see fit.

Some of the applications for virtual real estate in the metaverse include the sale of land for profit, the rental of land for passive income, the construction of different buildings such as online stores on existing property, and the hosting of social gatherings.

For instance, Decentraland, in conjunction with Adidas, recently organised a virtual fashion show where designs were auctioned off as non-fungible tokens (NFTs), serving as an example of the metaverse's digital real estate sector. Musicians are also taking an interest in virtual real estate, since it allows them to perform and sell National Football League tickets and products online.

The Metaverse's Long-Term Prospects

Even though they are still in the early phases of development, metaverses have the potential to provide a plethora of new social and financial possibilities via the usage of NFTs and new methods for people to communicate with one another congregate, to earn, and to trade.

Metaverses and NFT blockchain gaming will become integral parts of Web 3.0, an era in which real-world businesses expand into the digital space and users discover the versatility of such environments, thanks to the incorporation of virtual reality, video games, social media, and cryptographic elements.

NFT ownership, we feel, is essential in the coming metaverses and will open the door to a plethora of new possibilities. According to the company, interested users may utilise the Binance

NFT Marketplace to find, gather, and trade unique NFT assets while also traversing the metaverse.

Some of the most important things to understand about the Metaverse

Facebook recently rebranded as Meta, reflecting the company's increased emphasis on the "metaverse," and Microsoft has now revealed that it will also enter this market shortly.

In his proposal, Meta suggests that the metaverse will ultimately enable us to participate across educational, work, and social situations, while Microsoft seems to be concentrating its efforts for the time being on the virtual office environment.

However, the question remains as to what the metaverse is and to what degree we should put our faith in the image being offered to us as being important to our everyday lives.

The concept itself is not a new one. In his 1992 cyberpunk book Snow Crash, science fiction author Neal Stephenson invented the word "metaverse," describing a 3D virtual environment in which individuals, represented by avatars, might interact with one another and artificially intelligent entities.

Many individuals have attempted to impose their meanings on the metaverse, as they would with any grand vision of a future that has not materialised. If you are unfamiliar with the concept, it may be beneficial to grasp some of the characteristics expected from a metaverse.

1. A virtual world:

I believe that this is the most significant aspect of a metaverse. Exploring it using a computer, game console, smartphone, wearable technology, or other device, and taking in the 3D images and music along the way, would be a rewarding experience. Essentially, the notion is that by doing so, you will feel more present in the metaverse, and hence less present in the real world (where your body stubbornly remains).

2. Virtual reality.

This will need the use of a virtual reality headset. The idea behind this is that you get immersed in the virtual environment, which allows you to feel even more present – at least until you come across anything that is still part of your daily life, such as a coffee table.

3. Other individuals.

The metaverse is a social environment. There are a plethora of other individuals there, all of whom are represented by avatars. According to the report, some of these avatars might be bots, virtual agents, or other representations of artificial intelligence. You may hang around with the other folks or even do stuff together if you want to be social. Given Facebook's background as a social networking site, it seems probable that the social component will play an important role in the metaverse.

Because, for example, you may utilise gaze to indicate who you are addressing, supporters of the metaverse and some experts think communication may be more natural in the metaverse than it is with video conferencing (your avatar can turn its head to look at another person). Your avatar might potentially stroll up to someone else's avatar and sit next to them to initiate a discussion.

4. Persistence.

In other words, the virtual world is always there anytime you choose to visit it. It is possible to alter it by adding new virtual buildings or other things, and the modifications are permanent the next time you come. Taking up residence and becoming a part-owner may be an option for you. In the same way that social media relies on user-generated material today – your digital creations and personal tales — the metaverse will depend on your user-generated content.

5. Connection to the real world.

It is possible that, in certain metaverse visions, virtual objects in the virtual world are representations of real objects in the real world. Using a virtual drone in the metaverse to control an actual drone in the real world is an example of this. "Digital twins" are terms used to describe the relationship between the actual and the virtual worlds.

What can I accomplish in a metaverse, and how fast can I do it?

  Different organisations will most likely have their visions or even local copies of the metaverse, but they will all be linked in the same way that the internet is, allowing you to travel freely from one to the next.

It's conceivable that certain items will be more instantly attractive and useful than others, depending on their nature. Playing games would seem to be a logical progression, given that many players already love online gaming, and that certain games have already made their way into the metaverse to some extent.

Additionally, the thought of being able to socialise or meet with people while feeling as if you're really in the same room with them in person is intriguing - especially in these era of pandemics.

We don't have a good picture of what Meta's metaverse offerings will be like just yet. According to CEO Mark Zuckerberg, the announcement of the rebranding included several possible alternatives. According to some predictions, a hologram may emerge at a real meeting, or you could play chess with someone on the other side of the globe on a virtual chessboard overlaid on the actual world.

According to Facebook's vision, the metaverse will serve as our future interface to the internet. However, it remains to be seen whether we will be able to access all internet services through 3D virtual worlds and virtual reality headsets in the future.

Despite several huge firms' efforts to bring virtual reality headsets to market in recent years, including Facebook's acquisition of Oculus, they still look to be a rather specialised technology.

I believe that Facebook will need to be in this for the long haul, and that their vision of the metaverse will be several years away from being a (virtual) reality shortly.

A final observation

However, although Stephenson's initial vision of the metaverse was immensely thrilling, it also had many potential dangers, both in the online and real world, ranging from addiction to crime and the collapse of democratic institutions, among other things. It's worth noting that giant businesses controlled the vast majority of Stephenson's metaverse, with governments reduced to the status of mostly inconsequential paper-shuffling outposts.

Given the present conflicts between big companies and governments across the globe over privacy, freedom of expression, and internet hazards, we should take a close look at what sort of metaverse we want to build and who will be in charge of creating, owning, and regulating it, before moving forward with it.

7.   Metaverse and Cryptocurrency

It is important to understand that the metaverse does not have to incorporate blockchain to exist, but to make the ecosystem more equitable and more secure for all participants, blockchain will play a key role in its development. With the metaverse, humans will evolve as a fully developed digital species.

Crypto meets Metaverse

Digital assets and cryptocurrencies seem to be the most vertical imperative in driving the emergence of a true metaverse. Therefore, we hear and see NFTs everywhere.

Non-fungible chips are the first step in integrating individual ownership with digital resources. A non-fungible token (NFT) is a digital item that can be created (invented), sold or purchased on an open marketplace and owned and controlled by any individual user, without the permission or support of a centralized company.

For digital items to have real and lasting value, they must exist independently of an entity that can decide to delete or disable the item at any time. What NFTs enable for the first time is a decentralized digital representation and a digital ownership layer through which deficit, uniqueness, and authenticity can be transparently managed.

Therefore, cryptography can be the necessary cornerstone for metaverses.

Why know Metaverse?

There are many cryptographic projects that are trying to develop a complete digital ecosystem based on blockchain. And because it is based on blockchain, we can participate in projects by owning their chips. One of those projects that I admire these days is Decentraland.

Decentraland is a 3D space where you can build virtual worlds, play games, explore museums full of NFT art, attend live concerts, etc. It works in a standard web browser to give you access to cryptocurrency and NFT features. You can buy and sell properties, create and sell virtual art for art galleries or build worlds. Several companies have invested in land in Decentraland and some of them may be willing to pay qualified builders for its development.

Because of what we have said, it is easy to understand how the market for cryptocurrencies related to augmented reality is rapidly expanding. Investing in Crypto Metaverse tokens could prove to be extremely productive, so let's see which are the best ones currently available on the market.

Decentraland (MANA)

The Decentraland platform with MANA tokens allows its players to purchase portions of land and use them to build/realize what they most desire (concerts, recreational spaces, land used for car driving tests). The owners of these assets are able to get real gains generated by the value imported by all users who interact with them. MANA token holders also have the right to vote on any changes that are proposed for the system, since it is based on DAO (Decentralized Autonomous Organization) technology.

Where you can buy:

https://www.etoro.com

https://www.binance.com/it

Axie Infinity (AXS)

It is a game inspired by the Pokémon universe. In fact, players can buy through AXS tokens (NFT) small animals, breed them and make them fight each other. By completing the different activities proposed by the game, users can earn, invest or sell more AXS tokens. Axie Infinity works by operating on the Ethereum blockchain, connected to Ronin (a sidechain that lowers commission costs and speeds up transactions).

Metaverse Index (MVI)

This token allows investors to invest in the world of cryptocurrencies related to the Metaverse without participating in gaming activities or virtual gaming platforms. In fact, investors can leverage the MVI token as a true ETF for the Crypto Metaverse, capturing tokens that offer various services in virtual reality environments. However, the tokens must be developed on the Ethereum blockchain and their capitalization must be greater than $50 million.

The Sandbox (SAND)

This metaverse allows its users to create, sell, and purchase unique items for use within the game experience. It is based on three main components: VoxEdit (a tool used to create the unique items or turn them into NFT SAND), the Marketplace (where artists, leveraging blockchain technology can sell their creations), Gamers (those who bring the Metaverse to life through their avatars, interacting and operating in the virtual world along with other users). SAND is an ERC-20 token based on Ethereum blockchain.

Somnium Space (CUBE)

In Somnium Space it is possible to create, buy and exchange digital worlds and NFT resources. The peculiarity of this system, based on CUBE tokens, is the fact that before making purchases or exchanges, users can experience and try the virtual worlds created. It will be possible to dine in a restaurant designed by another player, or visit an exhibition in a museum. CUBE is also based on Ethereum blockchain and is an ERC-20 utility token.

8.   Metaverse, Marketing, Retail and E-commerce

Although this is a technology in the development phase, with projects that are still embryonic or that have not abstractly exploited all the possibilities offered by a metaverse, the attention to this world that combines the real with the virtual is very high among marketing and communication players as well as retail and eCommerce operators.

If the metaverse acquires the power to involve people that social networks have acquired since 2008, it is clear that we are facing the new frontier of virtual interaction, capable of revolutionizing the dynamics through which to promote a product or a service, acquire and retain customers.

In the metaverse coexist and integrate with each other: virtual shops, augmented reality, NFT, streaming services, information sites, video platforms, eCommerce portals and more.

The big digital players become the "creators" of digital worlds made of patents, software, platforms, collaborations, partnerships aimed at making people live a second life (or first life) in which they can transfer a substantial part of their daily life and preserve their identity.

Among the pioneers are large fashion companies. For example, Gucci with the virtual version of the Gucci Garden open to the public within the Roblox platform. Or again, Balenciaga with its skins for Fortnite.

Of interest for industrial development is the partnership concluded between Nvidia and BMW. The objective? The creation of a "virtual original" of a factory in order to virtually plan new workflows, before applying them to the physical factory. Here's another example of the potential of real-virtual interaction systems.

Not only. In an increasingly phy-digital market, where the shopping experience must be increasingly immersive, eCommerce and retail could see with the advent of the metaverse a further boost.

Imagine having a coffee with a friend of yours, sitting at a table in a coffee shop. You describe the t-shirt you would like to buy and in an instant a selection of t-shirts flashes in your peripheral vision. Digital images scroll by. Your virtual assistant, based on your preferences and thanks to artificial intelligence, fine-tunes your selection.

- And there's the t-shirt you wanted.
- With a simple gesture, you can buy the t-shirt and get (or purchase) an NFT version to dress up your holographic avatar.
- Say hello to your friend. You slip off your glasses.
- You've had coffee with a friend, purchased a t-shirt, all from the comfort of your couch at home.
- That's one of the potentials of the metaverse.

Merging the physical world with the virtual one, in order to significantly enrich the daily experiences of users.

The metaverse as a tool to offer greater access to consumers than today's material world. Or, the metaverse as a way to improve the eCommerce experience, responding to corporate and consumer needs. In other words, the speed of an online purchase, with the experience of an in-store purchase.

The eCommerce Metaverse: Instructions for Use
Since there is no single metaverse, it is not possible to provide unambiguous instructions.

Some rules of caution are, however, necessary.

Read the terms and conditions (if any) before creating your avatar and accessing the metaverse.

Do not provide sensitive and/or personal information, if you are not sure of the reliability of the platform or of the user-avatar you are interacting with.

Always remember that if you act as a consumer, there are more favorable rules.

This evolution of the tech giants will also strongly influence fashion and sales.

Since 2020, everything has moved into the realm of ether and virtual; fashion houses will be doing shopping experiences through glasses and viewers: you can comfortably shop and try on clothes from the couch at home

Thanks to the visor you will find yourself in the virtual world: you will be able to follow office meetings, go shopping, try on items from the new collection of your favorite designer or play.

It will be the triumph of secure shopping and customers will find virtual objects thanks to Blockchain and NFT technology and can easily access exclusive content: works of art, sports tokens collectibles.

In addition to Facebook there are Microsoft, Roblox, Epic Games, Tencent, Alibaba and ByteDance who have invested millions of dollars on the development of the project.

Mesh for Microsoft Teams will allow us to participate in video calls in avatar version even without glasses or visors: Microsoft's cloud will realize virtual reality by exploiting artificial intelligence.

Alibaba is working to prepare for the new virtual e-commerce, while ByteDance (which controls TikTok) is figuring out how to evolve video in 3D format.

Ayayi new fashion icon

Ayayi is the Chinese digital influencer so realistic that she looks real.

Lil Miquela, a virtual pop star as well as model and influencer, had appeared in 2020.

Ayayi is a "meta-human" influencer.

Influencer marketing is the main promotion tool in China for brands that want to conquer the market and the use of KOLs (Key Opinion Leaders) is one of the most efficient strategies.

The French maison Guerlain, a brand of perfumes, cosmetics and skin care products has expressed its willingness to collaborate with Ayayi.

The Metaverse, avatars and the virtual will be the future of fashion and not only.

Big giants have already understood this, but also luxury brands such as Gucci and Louis Vuitton.

The challenge will be to move from social networks to the virtual world, creating new sales channels and dressing in digital, in pixels and not in fabric.

A bet already faced by many, for example the capsule collection of Moschino for The Sims, that of the Metaverse will be a great challenge.

9.   Building The Metaverse Experience

Things are moving quickly, and if you want to stay up with your users and rivals, you will have to get started right now. Here's a fast selection of resources to help you learn more about the metaverse and how you can use the underlying technology to generate value for your brand.

3D Modelling

3D modeling is crucial to building metaverse experiences. Hence why this section is important. We have provided a detailed guide to help you refresh your 3D modeling knowledge or set you on the path of learning. Either way, there are tremendous opportunities for creators to develop experiences that will shape the future of metaverse. You want to pursue 3D modeling as a job or a pastime. We will show you how to get started.

3D modeling necessitates a unique blend of technical and creative abilities. It is a career-oriented field with a lot of promise, especially in the metaverse. 3D modeling offers a variety of applications that may be useful in the virtual world, and it is a talent worth learning.

While it is a frequent notion that the entry barrier is quite high, this is not the case. In reality, even if you do not like to put in a huge amount of money, it is not difficult to get started with 3D modeling today. You are ready to go as long as you have a computer with a good processor and some form of a graphics card.

The fundamental concept behind 3D modeling is to build three-dimensional shapes that can be viewed in various ways. The ultimate result may be a static scene generated from a certain angle or a complex model that can be viewed from any aspect.

When dealing with 3D, you normally begin with a simple geometric shape (such as a cube, sphere, or cylinder) and alter it using different modifiers until it matches what you attempt to create. Of course, that is an oversimplified version; most complicated models are made up of several smaller shapes adjusted separately.

The basic procedure is changing their shapes on several layers. You may either move the entire object around (or apply many other changes, such as resizing or rotating it). Alternatively, you can divide it into its constituent parts and deal with them individually.

When working with a cube, for instance, you can alter one of its sides. You may also deal with specific vertices or simply one edge of that side (the corner points that connect edges). Using different modifiers, you may quickly apply significant changes to such shapes.

Choice of 3D Modeling Software

3D modeling was often thought to be a discipline that needed sophisticated commercial software to enter. 3ds Max, Maya, Cinema 4D, Houdini, and other prominent software packages are still used today. Blender, the only effective free software, existed back then, but it was not the Blender that most of us are familiar with now.

In terms of functionality, UI/UX, simplicity of use, and community support, Blender may easily compete with the main leaders in the industry today. Several studios are now expressly looking for Blender expertise, which was not the case a few years ago.

With that in mind, Blender is the ideal option if you do not wish to spend a huge amount of money on commercial software. It is capable of taking you as far as other common options available on the market. Blender is expected to grow in popularity in the foreseeable future as the development of the virtual space continues.

3D Modeling Hardware Requirements

Hardware Requirements

One of the most common criticisms of 3D modeling is that it needs powerful gear to get started. That is no longer the case.

Modern 3D programs such as Blender can be operated on even a subpar PC with an incorporated graphics card. When dealing with sophisticated modifiers or when your scene becomes huge, editing may take a while, but you will not be doing any of that when you initially begin.

A faster computer immediately translates to quicker rendering speeds when it comes to rendering. This implies that if you have the time to wait for your renderings to complete, you can get away with a low-powered machine. Keep in mind that the speed differential might be fairly dramatic. A computer with a powerful graphics card, such as an RTX 3070, could render a scene in seconds, but an older system may take days.

There are internet rendering farms that could help with this, but they are not free. This is a better way than investing a few thousand dollars on a modern computer.

3D Modeling for Business

Suppose you have decided to pursue 3D modeling for business purposes, such as building a metaverse experience rather than just as a creative pastime. In that case, you will want to concentrate on a few key areas. Selling unique models is a fantastic place to start. However, it is a saturated field.

You might also consider selling your renderings to individuals and brands in other formats, such as conventional art (prints or t-shirts). To summarize, 3D modelers are in high demand in the metaverse development industry.

You should research the industry and identify the essential abilities you will need to succeed. In this sense, each area of 3D modeling is distinct, and you will have to spend some time experimenting until you find what you want to achieve.

Getting Started with 3D Modeling

Join various 3D modeling platforms if you have determined you are ready to pursue 3D modeling. One of the best things about 3D modeling is that the community is well-developed. There are usually plenty of individuals willing to assist you and address any problems you could have.

CAD Modelling

Installation

We will begin with the installation of the CAD software known as AutoCAD. AutoCAD is not a free program; it costs 185 dollars a month to subscribe. It costs $1775 per year. As a result, it is a little expensive. You do, however, have a choice. If you are a beginner, Autodesk provides a free trial. But, in my perspective, it is legal if you can buy this even for a short period.

Free trial

The free trial period will last 30 days. Free trials are available for the following options.

AutoCAD WIN/MAC

Architecture toolset WIN

Electrical toolset WIN

Map 3D toolset WIN

Mechanical toolset WIN

MEP Toolset WIN

Plant 3D toolkit WIN

Raster Design toolset WIN

AutoCAD mobile app

AutoCAD web app

AutoCAD 2020 System Requirements

- **Operating System: Microsoft Windows 10 (64-bit only), 8.1 (64-bit only), or Windows 7 SP1 (64-bit only)**
- Processor: 2.5 GHz (3+ GHz recommended)
- Memory: 8 GB (16GB recommended)
- Disk Space: 6.0 GB
- Displ1920 x 1080 resolution with True Color

Identify the User Interface

You may now launch AutoCAD after it has been properly installed. There is a user interface with a lot of buttons and text on it. Therefore, let us have a look at what you need to understand about this.

AutoCAD is mostly used for drawing. Beginners, on the other hand, may use this to begin 3D modeling. The rationale for this is that all of the fundamental commands can be learned quickly using real-life examples. Let us have a look at what is included in these interfaces.

Drafting and Annotation Interface

- Application Button

The application button can be used for a variety of file-related operations. In addition, the application button provides access to the printing and file exporting operation options.

- Toolbar for Quick Access

The quick access toolbar has features for quick save, print, open redo, and undo.

- The Ribbon Area

The ribbon area has a variety of tools. Line drawings, modification, and editing options are all found in the ribbon area when you're using the drafting interface.

- File Tabs

In this tab, you can see which files are open and which are being worked on.

- UCS

In 3D modeling, the User Coordinate System is the most significant factor. In AutoCAD, there are two major coordinates. Both the UCS (user coordinate system) and the WCS (world coordinate system) are used. Both may be altered depending on our needs and location. We may adjust the work plane and direction using them.

- Layout Tabs

The most often used layouts in AutoCAD are model and plotting layouts. These tabs allow you to switch between printing and working layouts swiftly.

- View Cube

The view cube contains all three-dimensional viewpoints. These are the views: front, back, top, left, right, and back. You may see the applicable view side of the item by simply clicking one side. You may see and view the model by clicking the edge.

- Navigation Bar

All navigation path processes are included in this. In this area, you may observe orbit, the navigation wheel, zoom function, and motion.

- Status Bar Toggle

This is a quick overview of the most often used drafting and annotation interface. This section handles all types of tracking (object tracking), workspace switching, and snap modes. You will understand more as your knowledge grows.

3D Modeling Interface
We will use this interface to learn more about 3D modeling. Only the ribbon and its choices may be changed here.

- Ribbon Tab

In the AutoCAD platform, the ribbon tab is the most often used tab for 3D modeling. This may be used for all types of solid and surface editing. The ribbon section allows you to do modeling, mesh editing, solid editing, drawings, altering, section editing, viewing, coordinates set, and layer management.

This is a quick rundown of the user interface. Let us look at how to make a simple 3D object now.

Fundamental Steps in 3D Modelling in AutoCAD
- Step 1: Decide on your units.

This is the very first thing you should do. Since you must be aware of the units on which you will be working. Millimeters, centimeters, meters, and kilometers are examples of standard units. So, you must choose which units you are going to focus on. After that, everything is modified accordingly.

- Step 2: Analyze the Model or Drawing

Before developing a 3D model, you must first examine the drawing, reference picture, or model and generalize the final product. When you examine it, you will notice that the same pieces are utilized several times and how the object's body should look from the front, rear, sides, top, and bottom, among other things.

What should the front look like, and how can it be seen from the sides? As a result, you must be familiar with the fundamentals of drawing—observations from the first and third angles. If you have done this before, you will be able to capture them in a matter of seconds.

- Step 3: Ideation

This section requires you to consider the final item. Which method should you use to get the object? The method should have the fewest steps possible, and the object should be 100% precise and rapid. Similar sections, mirrored parts, holes, tapering, bends, linkages, and other features can be seen during the examination. These types can be altered depending on the level of intricacy.

Separate modeling and putting them together can be preferable to modeling the entire item. As a result, you may extract various types of facts into your mind during the analysis phase. Everything should begin with drawing. So, stick with that for a more effective approach.

- Step 4 Modeling

Draw the picture first, then use 3D instructions to create and finish the object, according to the drawing you gave. In 3D modeling, the essential thing is to save and retain a copy.

- Step 5 Connecting Parts

In this stage, the different modeled objects are connected to form a single object. For a better tracking procedure, you may use snap tracking in this stage.

- Step 6: Finalizing

After modeling, create a "UNION" object to link all the connections and objects together. If the pieces are in distinct files, combine them before finalizing the project. If you use AutoCAD rendering, AutoCAD provides an excellent rendering solution appropriate for modeling objects.

- Step 7 Plotting

After completing all of the steps, you will need to plot, which we refer to as printing. In Auto-CAD, you may print in a variety of methods. The ideal method is outlined below.

Plotting in AutoCAD in the Easiest and Fastest Way
- **Select "Visualize" tab**

* Select "Model Viewports" and then "Name"
* Make a new view name in the viewport settings and then click "OK."
* Then, on the layout switching panel, "right-click" the "+" mark.
* Then, load the "New" or "Template" layout.
* Navigate to the fully loaded layout
* Go to the "Layout" panel in the loaded layout.
* Next, go to layout viewports and choose "Named"
* Select and load the stored name.
* You may show any view by drawing on the layout.

Photogrammetry

This section will walk you through the fundamental principles of the photogrammetry workflow that is required to create experiences in the metaverse. Photogrammetry is the act of getting exact measurements from images. It entails collecting a series of overlapping images of an item, structure, people, or environment and utilizing a variety of computer programs to turn them into a 3D model.

Applications of Photogrammetry

Photogrammetry is utilized in a variety of applications. We will walk you through some of the interesting applications of photogrammetry in the metaverse.

* **Artists can document or transform a previous work of art, sculpture, or natural phenomenon into something new.**
* Designers and engineers need to reverse design or custom-fit new pieces onto an old product.
* Photogrammetry mixed with semi-automatic 3D modeling processes can help game developers save time generating items and settings—a typical metaverse application.
* Artwork and artifacts in the sphere of cultural heritage can now be conserved indefinitely and digitally restored and repaired.
* Curators at museums can create virtual collections to entice visitors.
* Photographers now have an additional dimension with which to work.
* Companies that seek to provide a 3D printing service for their most valuable things, pets, or family members can now do this with photogrammetry.

These applications demonstrate the potential of the metaverse, and the opportunities abound for developers and brands.

Now let's delve deeper into the concept of photogrammetry and how to get started.

The Process of Photogrammetry
* Step 1: Take Images

Take a sequence of overlapping images of the thing you want to capture. For apps with low accuracy requirements, an 8-megapixel phone camera will suffice, but we suggest an 18 MP (or higher) DSLR-type camera for optimal results. The most recommended camera is a wide-angle camera as it has the least amount of lens distortion. A fish-eye lens, for instance, will not operate unless you use applications that can effectively correct it.

It is advisable to capture the images in a circle around the object. Begin with a low-angle circle, then repeat with a higher-angle circle to cover the topmost surfaces. Aim for a minimum of 50 percent overlap between every image, with 60-80 percent being optimum. Finally, take a couple more images of regions where crucial features can be found.

Take the following extra guidelines into consideration:

- **Ensure that the piece has a matte surface. Transparent items are difficult to transform. 3D scanning spray or dry shampoo spray could be used to turn reflective surfaces matte.**
- Many software programs struggle to deal with featureless surfaces. Surface scannability can be improved using shoe polish, sprayable chalk, painter's tape, and stone effect spray paint.
- The image's backdrop should have enough color contrast with the item. A chroma-key background or a newspaper, as long as it does not exhibit the same colors as the item, works well.
- Lighting must remain steady throughout the session, and a gloomy day is ideal.
- For a single object, 40-50 images are usually sufficient. The more images you take, the better, as long as you do not take them all from the same spot.
- The object must occupy a large percentage of the visual space.
- During the shot, be careful not to move the object.
- For every image, use a minimum depth-of-field (DOF) as possible and focus the camera precisely on the item.
- Use a tripod to prevent blurriness and for low-light situations that necessitate long exposure periods.

Based on the amount of the dataset, photogrammetry software programs might take hours or even days to deliver reliable results, even though they are continually improving. A machine with 16GB of RAM and an Nvidia CUDA-enabled GPU is required.

- Step 2: Upload

Open your preferred photogrammetry program and import the images straight into the project library. It is typically only a case of dragging and dropping. It is necessary to confirm the camera's compatibility for specific apps. They may cross-reference them with an internal database for the software to maximize its results depending on focal length, primary point, and image sensor format. A set of distortion variables referred to as a bundle adjustment are generated as a result of this.

The images will be examined for applicability to the photogrammetry procedure in the first phase of the software workflow. A green or red symbol, for instance, may show next to or on top of a picture in the library. If a large section of the photoset is declined and shooting a fresh batch is difficult, basic Photoshop manipulation might help. With white wall backgrounds, this is a regular occurrence. Creating a trash matte mask for every image helps to further differentiate the subject from the background. Refining the images may also help since the program will recognize similar characteristics across photos more easily if they are all of the same sharpness.

- Step 3: Using Photogrammetry Software to Create a 3D Model from Images

The photogrammetry program in the background handles the majority of the computational aspect of photogrammetry. However, additional functionalities may help enhance the results.

Image Matching

Many photogrammetry software packages convert the photoset into a 3D model completely automatically. On the other hand, some take Image Matching, sometimes referred to as Correspondence Search, as a distinct phase that the user must confirm. This enables changes to the photoset to be made before the more computationally demanding operations begin. The computer evaluates whether images are suitable for further processing and searches for overlapping regions in several images in this stage. It now saves how the photos will be stitched up, similar to how a 3D puzzle is put together.

Feature Extraction

This is, once again, a completely automated aspect of the photogrammetry operation in certain applications. It is possible to split this stage into various photogrammetry software applications for possible changes and iterations before proceeding. The program searches the images for traits that can be identified across numerous images in this stage. For this, some expert toolkits employ coded markers, a very precise solution that works on shiny, clear, and rather featureless surfaces. On the other hand, most tools employ the more generic Structure from Motion (SfM) method, which focuses on thick patterns on items like texts, wood grain, facial characteristics, and other designs. Edge points, lines, and corners are also essential elements. Some methods use an innovative system referred to as Shape-from-Shading to augment the data with lighting and shading signals.

In a process called Geometric Verification, they are internally validated to filter out false detections when all characteristics have been detected. The SfM engine provides a conversion that translates feature points between pictures to guarantee that the identified characteristics fall onto the same scene point. This is a sophisticated set of projective geometry-based algorithms.

Many photogrammetry applications, like COLMAP, enable users to observe the feature creation process in real-time. It is possible to halt the process in Meshroom if the user notices crucial locations where few characteristics have been discovered. Quality can be improved. By boosting keypoint sensitivity and matching ratio, adjusting presets, and converting the matching algorithm to A-KAZE or, in certain circumstances, a brute force technique.

Triangulation

In 1480, Leonardo Da Vinci invented a method for determining the painter's origin from an art piece. In this essential component of the SfM process, something occurs. The surface points' 3D coordinates are calculated using the scene graph generated from the previous phase. The ray cloud is created by reconstructing the lines of sight from the camera to the item. The junction of the multiple beams determines the object's ultimate 3D coordinates.

After establishing global geometry with a sparse point cloud, photogrammetry software creates a depth map by analyzing the lighting and texture of the environment. This, like a woodcarver, adds all the small touches to the 3D model to bring it to life. Advanced applications employ a technique called delighting in smoothening the illuminated and darkened portions for more homogenous lighting throughout the full surface of the model. It is even feasible to reverse-calculate ambient occlusion effects and clears them away. While a genuinely illuminated model is frequently preferred for on-screen display, a delit model is best for full-color 3D printing.

The depth map is referred to as dense reconstruction. The sparse reconstruction, which laid out all visual elements discovered previously, is then integrated into a 3D mesh format like FBX, OBJ, PLY, or STL.

The process of triangulation is carried out automatically. The user may improve the image quality by changing the Track Length, Number of Neighboring Cameras, and Maximum Points parameters. Many photogrammetry systems also let you know how many triangles are in a 3D mesh model, impacting file size and post-processing time. It is important to note that changing these variables should be done with caution because they might quickly increase processing times.

Many commercial photogrammetry software packages include extra machine learning approaches to categorize identified flora, structures, and automobiles. They can sift out moving background items like animals and people and create improved shape data based on foreground outlines, reflectivity, and brightness. Using the catenary curve fitting techniques, thin objects like steel frames and power lines may be automatically generated in 3D.

- Step 4 Post-Processing

While the analytical aspect of photogrammetry is complex, it is typically the most straightforward for the user, who simply has to drop in their photos and press a few buttons. When the 3D model has been created, the actual labor begins. Photogrammetry does not produce a waterproof mesh model that is suitable for 3D print. Floating art pieces, background sound, holes, and inconsistencies are all common issues to clear up. The item will equally need to be repositioned and resized, which photogrammetry software can perform at will.

Many software programs provide built-in post-editing capabilities; if not, a good approach is to complete the required file conversions in Meshlab and the mesh cleanup, mending, remeshing, and resculpting effort MeshMixer. This software is available for business usage at no cost.

The model will be set for 3D printing or import into a CAD system after this phase is completed and the file is stored in STL format.

LiDAR

Are you familiar with LiDAR technology? How would you feel if you could wave your magic wand and instantly know how far everything is from you? This is how LiDAR works.

After reading this, you should be on your way to becoming a LiDAR hero and start applying your skill to create the metaverse experience.

Meaning of LiDAR (Light Detection and Ranging)
LiDAR is a distance technology. LiDAR devices beam light to the ground from a plane or helicopter. The signal travels to the earth and then back to the sensor. The time it takes for the signal to return to the sensor is then measured.

LiDAR calculates a distance by tracking the time it takes for a signal to return. The word LiDAR (Light Detection and Ranging) comes from this.

How LiDAR Works
LiDAR is a technology for sampling. It puts out over 160,000 signals every second. Each 1-meter pixel receives roughly 15 signals per second. This is why LiDAR point clouds have such a large number of points.

Since LiDAR technologies are managed in a platform, they are extremely accurate. For instance, vertical precision is approximately 15 cm, and horizontal precision is only about 40 cm. LiDAR devices scan the ground from side to side while an aircraft flies through the air. While some signals may fall straight down at nadir, most will travel at an angle (off-nadir). As a result, when a LiDAR system estimates elevation, it also considers angle.

The swath width of linear LiDAR is generally 3,300 feet. New technologies such as Geiger Li-DAR, on the other hand, can scan widths of 16,000 feet. In comparison to traditional LiDAR, this sort of LiDAR can cover far larger footprints.

Possibilities on LiDAR

- Elevation Models

Digital Elevation Models are topographic models of the Earth's surface. You may create a DEM using solely ground returns. However, this differs from Digital Terrain Models (DTMs), which include contours.

You may create more items by utilizing a DEM. For instance, you might create:

Slope

Aspect (slope direction)

Hillshade (shaded relief considering illumination angle)

- Digital Surface Models

LiDAR, as you have learned, looks through the trees. The light ultimately hits the earth. Then we have a return to a bare Earth. However, what about the first return to the tree?

Elevations from natural and constructed surfaces are combined in a Digital Surface Model (DSM). For instance, it adds structures, tree cover, power lines, and others.

- Canopy Height Model

The real elevation of geographical objects on the ground is determined using Canopy Height Models (CHM). This form of elevation model is also known as a Normalized Digital Surface Model (nDSM).

Take the DSM, which comprises both natural and artificial characteristics such as trees and structures. Take out these heights from the naked Earth's surface (DEM). When you remove the two, you obtain a surface of elements that reflects true ground level height.

- Light Intensity

LiDAR intensity refers to the reflective percentage. Light intensity is influenced by range, incidence angle, beam, receiver, and surface material (in particular). However, light intensity is influenced by some things. When the pulse is angled further away, for instance, the return energy diminishes.

When it comes to recognizing characteristics in land use/cover, light intensity is extremely beneficial. In light intensity photographs, impervious surfaces, for instance, stand out. This is why picture categorization, such as object-based image analysis, benefits from the light intensity.

- Point Classification

The American Society for Photogrammetry and Remote Sensing (ASPRS) gives a series of classification codes to LiDAR point categorization.

Point categorization can often fall into more than one class. Ground, forest (low, medium, and high), structure, and water are examples of these classes. Vendors frequently mark these places with supplementary classes if this is the case.

LiDAR may or may not be classified by vendors. The codes are created semi-automatically by the reflected laser pulse. This LAS categorization field is not included in all manufacturers' packages. It is normally agreed upon in advance of the contract.

Components of the LiDAR system

A LiDAR has four primary components. They collaborate to provide extremely precise and practical results:

- LiDAR sensors: Sensors on the airplane scan the earth from side to side as it moves. Typically, the signals are in the green or near-infrared wavelengths.
- GPS receivers: GPS receivers monitor the airplane's height and location. These traces are critical for obtaining correct topography and elevation data.
- Inertial measurement units (IMU): IMUs track the tilt of planes as they move. Tilt is used in LiDAR technology to determine the signal's incidence angle properly.
- Data recorders: A device records all of the signal returns while LiDAR scans the surface. These data are then converted to elevation.

10. Risks and Challenges

As it is with any new, big ideas, there are bound to be issues that arise, whether direct or indirect. In the case of the rise of the metaverse and wanting to be a part of it all, there are also some risks and challenges of which to be made aware. Some of these risks are quite similar to issues that we can already see with the Internet and social media, and others are completely new. As for challenges, developers will face many difficulties in building the technology that this innovative platform requires in order to seamlessly integrate itself into the lives of the masses, just as the Internet had done a couple decades ago.

Social Risk

Addiction

With all the advancements of the digital world, people—and, in particular, youth—find themselves drawn to technology. Therapists now deal with thousands of children who are, at various levels, so indoctrinated to their devices that, to varying degrees, they cannot live in the real world normally. With the rise of the Internet and all the good it brought with it, also came new problems, and one such is that of addiction. Whether Internet Addiction Disorder (IAD) qualifies as a true mental illness, however, remains a hot debate.

In 2016, Common Sense Media, a nonprofit organization designed to provide reviews of technology and movies for families, discovered from a survey that around 50% of teenage participants felt "addicted" to their phones, and that 75%of these people felt the urge to immediately reply to notifications (Robb, 2016). However, most of these individuals would not be using the word "addiction" in the same way as substance abuse may make a person chemically addicted by altering the brain. True addiction would be to push out everything else from that person's life, not being able to function normally socially or physically, and need an increasing amount of the substance as time progressed. This is much rarer when it comes to the Internet, which is why it is often not classified as causing "addiction."

This being said, there are children who are deeply affected by the amount of screen-time they receive. Some children arrive in therapy clinics because they truly can no longer tell the difference between what is real and what is virtual. However, even this is debated as whether or not the effects were truly caused by access to the online realm, since these children may also have other underlying issues or disorders that have passed unchecked, and this in combination with screen-time has brought to light new symptoms. Either way, the best way to understand a child who the parent feels spends too much time on technology is to consult professionals in psychology and child therapy.

So, why are online games, media, and apps so addicting? Well, this is by design; the more time users spend on a platform, the more money that platform can potentially make either from advertisements, in-app purchases, or by other methods. Video game companies often specifically create "compulsory loops" that make the player want to continue playing on and on. Expectation, leading to reward, releases dopamine in the brain and makes the user feel good, which also leads to them wanting to continue using the technology (Smith, n.d.). Examples of rewards could be completing a level of a video game or getting "likes" on a social media post as a sort of validation. The inconsistency and dependency on the user to achieve these rewards also makes the experience more exciting, thus increasing dopamine.

The metaverse plans to make technology more interactive and more lifelike than ever. It will also not only boost social media activity but will encourage people to spend even longer periods of time on its platforms than even the modern Internet. There is thus the high risk of increasing dependency on technology, especially by the youth, whose minds are still moldable and underdeveloped. This posts the social risk of new generations that will not be able to function outside of the virtual world as easily as the generations that did not have virtual and augmented reality integrated into their early lives.

The issue becomes even more nuanced in debate: Is this truly a problem with the industry, that purposely makes their technology addicting in order to keep user retention? Or rather, is this risk, instead of placing the blame on the metaverse or the Internet itself, a responsibility of parental management? After all, it is the parents who decide how much screen-time a child receives, and it is the parents who buy the devices. In this way, it can be debated that parents should be responsible for how their child interacts with technology.

Social Media
When looking out at the future of the metaverse, the social media world only seems to improve, becoming more interactive and easily accessible than ever. As mentioned, however, addiction may also become more rampant. Additionally, there is a significant challenge in successfully transferring an already large and established user database to a whole new platform. Finally, many of the problems that modern social media faces, such as concerns of privacy or safety, will not simply disappear by, say, innovating the technology that it uses or changing the name of the company.

First of all, the addiction to social media has already been touched upon; that idea of "likes" on a post releasing dopamine to the account owner. However, unlike some iPad games or browsing movies and videos, social media does have a very strong connecting aspect, bringing together people from around the world who would have never met otherwise, and allowing them to talk, exchange ideas, and learn from each other. In this case, the main issue is not something so easily overcome. The idea of FOMO, that is, **fear of missing out**, has been amplified, since people feel they **have** to keep up with all the memories of their friends, for fear of being left in the dark to something interesting. In the metaverse, where there will be so much more to see, FOMO sentiments will definitely only increase.

The challenge of transporting an established user base to another platform will be further explained in the **Developers' Challenges** part of this section, however it remains a social risk that the metaverse will inevitably undertake. In the most relevant current case, Meta is already seeing issues in its rebrand. Their main website, Facebook, still remains the face of the company, and therefore, as it stands, nobody really associates Mark Zuckerberg with the word "Meta" at all, except maybe in a mocking sense. Something similar happened in the past with another big company, Google, which, in 2015 renamed its parent company to Alphabet, Inc. in order to expand further than being a search engine. Just like with Meta, though, to the general public, the company is referred to as Google since most consumers don't care about the bureaucracy of the organization.

Finally, problems that social media presently face may be amplified with the dawn of the metaverse. Facebook was under fire when it announced its rebrand to Meta, since many critics speculated this change was in large part due to the infamy associated with the current name. Facebook had become notorious for selling the personal information of their users to large corporations in order to send them tailored, personalized ads. This was all done with the false promise that consumers would be able to have control over how their information was shared by sifting through settings. So, the world went crazy when Facebook rebranded, and it seemed like just that: changing the name so as to dissociate from bad press without actually making any underlying changes. How can one thus expect companies to act any differently—especially when it pays so handsomely—when the metaverse will just require even more personal information from users, as it truly becomes a virtual self.

This is not the only issue with social media that will be transferred to the metaverse. Internet safety has been a widespread concern since it first came online. That people can pretend to be whomever they want is a frightening thought: anyone with whom you have an online conversation could be completely different in real life to how they present themselves therein. With Facebook, measures have been taken to try and avoid this at all costs, since it undermines the very principles on which it was founded, by vetting all accounts to make sure that they are run by real people providing their real information, which is, as has just been discussed, a whole different issue in itself, but works to keep out bot-run profiles. Other metaverse platforms cannot be expected to take the exact same measures as one company, and so this begs the question: if you get attached to a life-like holographic persona in the virtual realm, and you discover that it is all falsified with malicious intent, then this would be even more damaging and harder to discover than it would be on the current Internet.

Environmental Risk

The environmental risk of the metaverse lies in blockchain mining, and one of the main concerns of developers should be to find a way to completely base the process on clean, reusable, sustainable energy if they have hopes of bringing their wide-scope dream to life.

The Developers' Challenges

Coding and Engineering

There have already been significant advancements not only in sandbox-like environments as is the case with games like Minecraft or Roblox, but also in AR and in cryptocurrency dapps—platforms like Ethereum allow direct coding straight onto the blockchain. However, this practice of blockchain coding is not so widespread or well-known as of late. That blockchain coding is quite difficult and that developers must confront their personal morality on the unsustainable qualities of their work are all risks that the metaverse must overcome in order to grow.

Growing to Be the Next Internet

In order to grow to be the next bigger and better Internet, which is the end goal of all this metaverse talk, there are many challenges along the way. The biggest one may be that of transferring established user bases to a whole new, different platform, in particular consideration of the demographic of those databases. Other difficulties include: keeping the platform decentralized, creating interoperability, and monetary issues.

Facebook remains the most popular social media platform as of 2021, however fewer youth under 18 are signing up. The demographic from 19 to around 25 years of age is the largest, and this tapers down as age increases, but it was found that many people of middle-age or older create accounts every day. Since Facebook has turned into a more adult-minded platform in general, there is some risk involved in sudden change, especially considering that VR demographics—those for whom the metaverse truly excites—are mostly young adults (Digital in the Round, 2021). These Facebook users already feel at home with the current face and it is difficult to imagine them so readily accepting a complete change in the norm.

Another difficulty that developers of the metaverse face is that age-old struggle of digital communities in keeping the system decentralized. With so many companies seeing the value and the monetary opportunity in control of the metaverse, in order to maintain balance, there must be no single power or authority of the virtual playground.

With the concept of decentralization also arises interoperability, a necessary advancement in technology that must be made in order to establish the fundamentals of a viable metaverse. Interoperability relates to a user being able to move from one app to another with the same avatar and profile. This has to be a collective effort from developers of all metaverse projects, since they all have to together find a way to let a user travel between their platforms whilst retaining their same profile.

Finally, the metaverse is **expensive**. If some virtual worlds want to be realistic in order to be more attractive to the first-time consumer, the cost of digital assets is high. This is perhaps why the involvement of such a big company as Meta is exciting for some of those pursuing the metaverse: it is a big source of funds. Still, monetary challenges also remain as a boundary for hopeful developers who would otherwise love to try their hand at coding for the platform of the future. There is so much work to get the idea of lifelike social avatars to interact in a way that is not so completely artificial as well. On platforms that already exist like **Second Life**, player avatars do not provide the same freedom of movement as a real person simply because all actions must be coded and animated. To further and further approach life-likeness, coding and animating budgets are bound to become more expensive as well.

11.　What Will the Metaverse Change?

The metaverse is not only bound to change the world as we know it but the way we view it. With the implementation of 3D worlds, we will have infinite possibilities for work, travel, entertainment, and more. Let's have a look at some of the ways we will use the metaverse in the future.

Travel

The metaverse will play an important role in travel in the future. Putting on our glasses will allow us to see anywhere on earth without having to travel. The world of 3D modeling and rendering has changed drastically over the past decade. In the past, rendering and shading realistic 3D models was extremely resource-intensive, and the results were heavy graphics. Nowadays, not only do we have better 3D production methods, but our graphic cards and internet connection also process them much more quickly and efficiently.

Leading companies like Unity and NVIDIA are already developing cutting-edge 3D graphic technologies that look extremely realistic. These graphics are currently used mainly in video games, but they are gradually making their way to the movie industry. Eventually, we will have video services that will allow us to travel anywhere in the world. Better yet, we won't have to deal with crowded landmarks and may choose any weather we like.

There will be more than just real-time travel in the metaverse. One of the most exciting features of the metaverse will be time travel. Though technically we will only travel to the past we know, it is a start. Imagine traveling to the "Seven Wonders of the Ancient World" or interacting with prehistoric hunter-gatherers. The possibilities are endless.

Metaverse travel will be perfect for those who love travel but can't due to certain limitations. Professionals who work full-time and have limited time off, parents who cannot travel with young children, elderly people who have physical limitations, and people with disabilities are examples of lives the metaverse travel will change.

Entertainment

The entertainment industry is about to undergo one of the greatest changes with the upcoming metaverse. We can expect the entertainment industry to become much more interactive and accessible.

For example, the metaverse can change the way we listen to music. Artists can create music videos in the metaverse and sell tickets to their studio sessions. In addition, the size of the venue won't matter for ticket sales. The metaverse can take live concerts to the next level. We won't be restricted to a specific time or place to watch our favorite artists, and we certainly won't have to wait for our favorite bands to go on tour.

This is also true for the movie industry. Our favorite movies and television series can easily be metaverses on their own. You could ride a dragon beside Daenerys Targaryen in the Game of Thrones metaverse or enter the Matrix for the ultimate **metaverseception**. We might see a scenario like this in the latter stages of the metaverse, but interactive movie experiences are likely to be available in the initial stages. Companies like Disney and Lucas Arts already own the intellectual property rights to their universes, so they are in a good position to create a metaverse based on their franchises.

Adult entertainment is another example that is expected to benefit from the metaverse. Some experts claim that the adult industry is expected to reach $122 billion in 2026. The introduction of new internet technologies to adult entertainment is nothing new. There are many websites offering video clips and webcam interactions to their customers. The adult entertainment industry has proven to be crisis-proof, and the metaverse is sure to add its own twist to it.

Another industry that is enthusiastic about the metaverse is the gambling industry. In 2021, online gambling generated $230 billion and remained one of the most lucrative markets for online enterprises. Decentral Games, for example, offers virtual gambling using NFTs and their DG coin. We can anticipate this trend becoming more popular as the metaverse expands.

Military

The military is one of the few low-profile investors in the metaverse. Keeping up with the latest technology is a necessity for the armed forces to stay in top shape. In addition, armed forces around the world rely on simulations to train their personnel. Because the metaverse will create realistic simulations, it is only natural for the military industry to take advantage of it.

Optimus System was one of the first companies to jump on board. Their company develops and supplies military training simulators. DEIMOS, their new metaverse technology, is preparing to enter the global market. Their system creates military training environments like precision shooting, tactical behavior training, and observation training. Optimus System CEO Nam-Hyuk Kim said: "We plan to expand the development of scientific products to implement more effective, real war-like training systems based on the technologies of the fourth industrial revolution. Our company will lead the global Metaverse market with new ideas and differentiated technologies."

Military war games and training cost organizations like NATO billions of dollars every year. With the help of metaverse technologies, not only would they be able to reduce their budget, but they could also create highly realistic training scenarios without endangering personnel.

E-commerce

Web 2.0 has made e-commerce a part of our everyday lives. Numerous business owners transitioned to digital, and countless others developed lucrative side businesses via e-commerce stores. Online deliveries have become the norm and kept the world going during the Covid-19 pandemic.

We can expect our online shopping habits to evolve with the arrival of the metaverse. The stores can create their own metaverses or come together to create virtual shopping malls. We can walk into these stores and check out the real size, color, and fit before we make the purchase.

On the other side of the metaverse, shopping will take place in the virtual reality economies themselves. Virtual land, tokens, and other goods unique to each metaverse will be available to us with cryptocurrencies. Currency for a metaverse can be Bitcoin, altcoins, or a completely original token.

Whatever the case may be, the metaverse will have a business opportunity in e-commerce. By deciding on the type of products you want to sell early on, you will have the opportunity to be among the first to enter the market. So, if you have an original idea or product, you should consider patenting it.

Workplace

Several tech giants like Microsoft have been working on creating a metaverse for the workplace. The initial plan is to create virtual conference rooms where colleagues could meet using virtual reality. During the pandemic, online meetings have already become commonplace in the workplace using apps like Zoom and Google Hangouts. Employees have felt the effects of what's called "Zoom fatigue," and companies are looking for better ways to engage employees online.

Through the metaverse, an online conference room will become much more realistic. The presentations will be more compelling, communication will feel more genuine, and the audience will be more engaged.

As metaverse workplaces prove to be useful, they could greatly increase the number of international teams. Furthermore, companies can hold their international meetings online and reduce their business travel expenses. Although the metaverse cannot completely replace human interaction, it can certainly speed it up. You can create a business that offers an international working hour scheduling service or create a translation plugin for international meetings. That is two excellent business models for the metaverse right there.

Gaming

Gaming will be one of the industries to cross the frontier into the metaverse. Virtual reality glasses caught the attention of the gaming industry when they were introduced. These days, popular game engines like Unity 3D offer developers to export their games for virtual reality. Moreover, 3D art and environments have been used in the industry for decades. We can expect game developers to be among the first to adapt to the upcoming metaverse.

They will be able to adapt quickly beyond the technical aspects of game development. Games with large followings, such as MMORPGs and MOBAs, have utilized their own currencies for in-game purchases for a long time. A few developers are now accepting cryptocurrency payments too.

The gaming industry has all these advantages over other industries, making it one of the poster children for Web 3.0. You can invest in the metaverse early on by investing in game studios that are shifting towards it. If you are a high-risk investor, look for angel investment opportunities in small startups. To be on the safe side, look for established game studios that are showing signs of making the shift. Collect stocks early and follow them regularly to ensure they are progressing.

Dating and Relationships

Online dating has changed the way we meet people many years ago. Nowadays, meeting someone is as simple as logging onto a website or downloading an app on your phone. We can only anticipate the metaverse to shake things up even more.

Remember that artificial intelligence and machine learning are crucial parts of Web 3.0. Dating applications like Tinder and OkCupid are wildly popular because they match us with people we're already interested in. This not only saves us time but increases the chances of a first date going well.

We can expect to see this on a larger scale once the metaverse starts influencing the dating world. Artificial intelligence will make smart guesses about our preferences. Whenever we express a liking or disliking for a specific trait, our choices will create a compound pool of characteristics we will be interested in.

We will be able to meet these people right away in the metaverse, which is even more exciting. Using this technology, we will be able to interact with people deeper without having to share personal information like phone numbers and addresses. This should make online dating a safer experience in the future.

Another group that will benefit from metaverse dating is long-distance couples. Some couples start off long-distance, and some evolve into long-distance relationships due to work like army officers. The metaverse era will give these people a chance to skip the Skype call and spend meaningful time with their loved ones.

Do you have a Christmas tradition of watching a certain holiday movie? Even when you are thousands of miles away from your loved ones, you can join the metaverse and watch the movie together. It doesn't end there. You can teach your children how to play chess, take your spouse on a two-hour date to Paris, and catch up with your friends on a virtual pick-up game. In the metaverse, you can do all of this and much more.

Media

Previously, we discussed the impact of information decentralization. One of the biggest industries to be affected by information decentralization was, undoubtedly, the mainstream media. Newspapers and news channels initially viewed the internet as a way to spread their accessibility. However, they took one of the biggest hits in the process.

Information democracy brought by the internet allows users to both generate and consume the information they want. Among the biggest reflections of this statement are the social media apps we use every day. Furthermore, the internet gives alternative media a fair chance to compete with mass media. As a result, the press no longer has a monopoly. A similar situation applies to big TV networks that have lost market share and influence to streaming services like Netflix.

It is hard to predict what Web 3.0 will bring to the table as far as the media is concerned. Web 3.0 is about us being able to see our input reflected back to us. Media outlets on the entertainment side might find it easier to adapt to Web 3.0. However, it remains unclear how the 24-hour news cycle will interact with Web 3.0. Governments will no doubt take action against the complete decentralization of news, as they do today. However, it can be speculated that self-journalism and social media will become more prominent. We will likely have more access to personal news stories that artificial intelligence thinks we will be interested in. In addition, there could be ways to set trigger alerts or mental health precautions based on what we consume. To date, Time has taken the boldest step into the metaverse from a media outlet. They are launching a weekly newsletter solely dedicated to the metaverse.

Education

The Covid-19 pandemic has proven that face-to-face education is not the only way to learn. While online education has its own challenges and setbacks, the metaverse can offer solutions. Using the metaverse, teachers can interact with children in virtual reality, which is a far cry from a Zoom call. Even more impressive, a teacher can instruct any student in any part of the world by means of machine learning techniques and translation technologies.

The metaverse has the potential to revolutionize education. Imagine yourself sitting in your Seattle home and taking a leisurely stroll in front of the Eiffel Tower with your favorite French teacher. Taking a school trip to Germany to learn about World War II without getting on a plane. Learn painting from Leonardo Da Vinci himself. Observing the human body from inside. These are a few examples of what virtual reality and artificial intelligence can do for the education system.

We can expect schools throughout the world to have metaverse campuses in the future. A few examples are already underway. A virtual campus will be created, for instance, at the Kenya-KAIST campus, which is expected to open by September 2023 in the Konza Technopolis. The University of Nicosia is preparing to open the first permanent university gallery for NFTs. They will also start offering a six-week course "Introduction to NFTs and the Metaverse," which starts in February 2022 as a part of their UNIC Open Metaverse Initiative. Over time, these examples will multiply and become more complex, resulting in student exchange programs being a daily occurrence.

Another group that will benefit from the educational implementation of the metaverse is students with disabilities. As a means of bridging the education gap between able-bodied and disabled students, augmented reality will be invaluable. It will be easier for teachers to design personalized activities for disabled students, and long-term hospitalization will not hinder academic success as much.

There is no doubt the metaverse will impact all industries one way or the other. What matters is how we respond to it. By embracing the metaverse early on and exploring its potential, we can take advantage of this wonderful technology and not let it pass us by as it changes the world.

12. A Step-By-Step Guide To Purchasing Real Estate In The Metaverse

Through a combination of augmented reality (AR), virtual reality (VR), and video, Metaverse is a step toward digitizing the actual world. Users can work, play, and communicate with pals in the virtual world using their digital avatars in the virtual universe. There are many things to do in the metaverse, from organizing a meeting to taking a virtual globe tour.

On the other hand, real estate appears to be capturing investors' attention. With unprecedented million-dollar purchases reported every other week, the volume of property deals in the metaverse has been making headlines.

To purchase virtual property, you must first register with a metaverse platform such as Decentraland, The Sandbox, or Axie Infinity, among others. Then, to transact in the metaverse, all you need is a well-funded digital wallet. Then, you can store your dollars in your digital wallet by converting them to cryptocurrencies like ether or native currencies of the metaverse you're transacting in, like MANA or Sandbox.

You may buy, rent, flip, or even sell homes in the digital world with the support of the metaverse's nearly full ecosystem, and ownership is based on non-fungible tokens (NFTs).

The following is a step-by-step guide to purchasing real estate in the metaverse.

1. Visit one of the metaverse's property marketplaces, such as Decentraland, Axie Infinity, or Sandbox, and log in.
2. Compare the prices of the various parcels of land that are available.
3. After you've chosen the digital plot of land you want to buy, click on it to learn more about it. It's vital to remember that a specific metaverse property platform will only enable you to buy from them if you use their approved cryptocurrency. Decentraland, for example, exclusively allows users to buy and sell homes with MANA, the company's cryptocurrency.
4. The next step is to connect your digital wallet to your account on the property site. To do so, you'll need to first obtain a suitable digital wallet. Metamask is the most popular digital wallet on the market right now. In addition, it's compatible with practically every metaverse property platform.

5. It's critical to fund your digital wallet with a cryptocurrency that works with the digital property platform you've chosen. Then, you may easily buy it on various exchanges and keep the cryptos safe in your digital wallet. All you have to do now is press the 'purchase' button when you've finished picking the land and funding your associated digital wallet.

6. Once you've completed the transaction, the digital land you've purchased is stored in your associated digital wallet as NFTs. So, in your digital wallet, go to the 'NFTs' page to see your newly bought land.

What you should know before buying metaverse real estate

Unlike investing in the real estate market, where your purchased physical land is guaranteed to survive, digital land in the metaverse will become non-existent if the platform you purchased fails and goes down. Another thing to remember is the significant volatility of the cryptocurrency used to transact in the metaverse's real estate market. Because the value of digital money fluctuates, the value of the metaverse property you possess fluctuates accordingly.

Furthermore, because digital real estate is a relatively new asset class, many facets have yet to be explored. As a result, investing in the metaverse's digital real estate market is very speculative; thus, thoroughly researching the advantages and downsides is recommended before making any decisions.

13. Ethics in the Metaverse

A major source of worry in the Metaverse is how to prevent toxicity or poor conduct in which people harass or intimidate others. Because many will be in the metaverse, it is obligatory upon its builders to make it a safe area for everybody. For example, people's opinions about sexuality might alter throughout time.

The difficulty had also evolved since, when we initially began with these internet experiences, whether virtualized or not, they did not incorporate as much of the actual world as they do now. The situation has changed. The Metaverse will soon be more like being in the actual world. We have to go through issues that no one else has gone through.

People will act if they see the metaverse as an add-on to reality rather than reality itself. Non-player characters may become more realistic, or perhaps smarter, in the future. According to Bartle, they may exhibit self-awareness. This might happen in the next few years, taking quantum computing to accomplish.

This poses a slew of ethical concerns. Are you going to eliminate the AI folks by erasing the database or turning it off? You might be able to resurrect them or at least duplicate them. Or do you destroy them by copying them? Have you become a mass killer if you develop a virtual environment for the sole purpose of killing characters?

You will then select the universe you want to visit, social or gaming realms. We will see a slew of small worlds or metaverses. A translation mechanism might be used to transport objects across Metaverse worlds.

You have to respect your players. Because you cannot leave the actual world if you do not like it, you will not be able to travel to another world where you do not have white hair. You have no choice but to remain in this reality. However, reality necessitates competition. You can always "go" to someone else's world if world operators surround you. You will have to respect them, or they will end up playing for someone else.

Simply, players want a place where they can be happy and be their best versions. In the physical world, the dice roll defines you. You do not have to be yourself in the virtual environment. You can uncover who you truly are. That is the kind of thing you would like to be able to see in the future.

Protocol Requirement Solution

With so many possibilities in the Metaverse, it is no surprise that so many technological behemoths continue to spend substantially on its growth. Because of the enormous potential influence, many people feel that this will be the next large-scale technology after the internet.

However, creating the "next internet" is easier said than done. Technical support for multiple dimensions and purposes, such as the ideal business economy, payment system, website economy, and other Web 3.0 aspects, is necessary to create the Metaverse.

As a Polkadot-based cross-chain protocol, X Protocol intends to fill this need. Polkadot (DOT) is a system that enables multiple blockchains to communicate similarly to the traditional internet by connecting different networks using Wanchain's decentralized bridges, a blockchain network interoperability framework. X Protocol thinks that by utilizing these elements, they will realize their goal of creating a "decentralized Metaverse based on Web 3.0."

To enter the Metaverse, the X Protocol Leverages Web 3.0. The protocol will establish a fair and decentralized standard for all economic activity while ensuring that any firm can freely distribute content. As a result, users may compare the X Protocol public chain to Ethereum (ETH), a blockchain well-known for its smart contract capabilities.

According to X Protocol, the focus has shifted to the basic layer one infrastructure, which comprises source-generated games and lands models. The project is written in RUST and revolves around the Polkadot and Solana (SOL) environment, comprising the protocol and application layers. The layers' major goals are to get organic traffic in the metaverse using self-developed decentralized apps (DApps) and give third-party DApps zero-barrier access to technological solutions.

X Protocol intends to produce DApps to attract organic users, then incorporate each DApp via Metaverse scenarios and give third-party DApps easy access to them; this will eventually result in a metaverse environment with a massive number of participants use cases. On Polkadot and Solana, X Protocol is rated one of the top metaverse projects in a group experience, linked wallets, and GitHub code volume.

On the X Protocol, a DeFi cross-chain asset pool is being constructed so that tokens generated on many blockchains may be freely exchanged irrespective of which chain they originate from. The X cross-chain bridge may be used to implement this swap capability on the platform. The X Protocol team believes that their approach will "significantly lower the transaction barrier" and "enhance the trading experience for users."

Conclusion

Suppose you are still trying to wrap your brain around virtual reality, augmented reality, mixed or extended reality ideas. In that case, it is time to move on because more tech firms are talking about a new era of the internet known as the Metaverse.

Despite its ambiguous definition, the word "Metaverse" is commonly used to express the idea of a future iteration of the internet consisting of shared, 3D virtual places linked into an imagined virtual world. In basic terms, the Metaverse is a virtual environment where you may use avatars to interact with other individuals in different geographical locations. Tech firms are considering various sorts of metaverse platforms. Users will buy land and develop ecosystems using NFTs and cryptocurrencies on a blockchain-based platform. A robust virtual environment where individuals may work, play, or interact could be another sort of platform. However, creating a Metaverse will rely heavily on AI and machine learning, as the metaverse's goal will be to combine our physical world with the virtual space via avatars. The Metaverse will be the convergence of virtual and augmented reality.

The Metaverse development will affect every facet of our civilization, especially entertainment, advertising, and the economy. The Metaverse, however, will have legal ramifications. Collaboration and interoperability between metaverse developers will be one concern. Intellectual property rights will be another issue, which is the case with most virtual products.

Even if the Metaverse currently falls short of the long-term vision that many have for it, it has the potential to alter how we interact with the virtual environment dramatically. A collaborative virtual experience, similar to NFTs, might open up new options for creators, gamers, entrepreneurs, investors, tech firms, and artists, not only restructuring but inventing the digital economy.

Whether it's a 2D web page or a 3D virtual world, the action of a widely recognized, representative, and authoritative organization to impose a reference standard with the participation of the main public and private stakeholders is essential. It is said that the meta-universe will belong to everyone, but at the same time, everyone is rushing to develop to seek a competitive advantage.

It should also be noted that the W3C era has undergone profound changes. Thirty years ago, it was in everyone's interest to create an environment that would allow new businesses to develop; no one would have thought that the Internet would get us where we are today, completely subverting social and economic patterns on a global scale.

The revolutionary momentum of the Internet has gradually given way to the dominance of large technology companies that occupy a strong position and are absolutely interested in creating new business platforms but will not risk losing the hegemony they enjoy. On the other hand, the government lags because technology continually works faster than regulatory design.

Aware of the risks and opportunities that will arise, it is necessary to find a basic condition of balance to make the metaverse a real development opportunity for all and the real manifestation of the dystopian scenarios described far.

Thank you for making it to the end of this book; we hope it has been informative and able to provide you with all the tools you need to achieve your goals, whatever they may be.

This book has tried to highlight all the important points so that you have a general and, in some cases, even specific knowledge about what will be the future of the Internet and all of society in the 21st century, so that you can benefit early from the future technological revolution while limiting its negative effects.

I hope this book will really help you achieve your goals.